D1539229

TRUTH & POWER

J.I. PACKER

TRUTH & POWER

THE PLACE OF SCRIPTURE IN THE CHRISTIAN LIFE

Harold Shaw Publishers
Wheaton, Illinois

All Scripture quotations, unless otherwise indicated, are taken from *The Holy Bible: New International Version*®. NIV®. Copyright © 1973, 1978, 1984 by the International Bible Society. Used by permission of Zondervan Publishing House.

Scripture quotations marked KJV are from the *King James Version* of the Bible.

Scripture quotations marked NEB are from *The New English Bible*, © The Delegates of Oxford University Press and The Syndics of the Cambridge University Press, 1961. Reprinted with permission.

Scripture quotations marked RSV are from the *Revised Standard Version* of the Bible, copyright 1946, 1952, 1971 by the Division of Christian Education of the National Council of the Churches of Christ in the USA, and used by permission.

ISBN 0-87788-815-9

Cover design by David LaPlaca

Library of Congress Cataloging-in-Publication Data

Packer, J. I. (James Innell)
    Truth and power : the place of Scripture in the Christian life / J.I. Packer.
        p. cm.
    ISBN 0-87788-815-9 (cloth)
    1. Bible—Evidence, authority, etc. 2. Bible—Inspiration. 3. Bible—Use.
    4. Bible—Influence. I. Title.
    BS480.P25 1996
    220.1—dc20   96-12562
                                                                 CIP

03 02 01 00 99 98 97 96

10 9 8 7 6 5 4 3 2 1

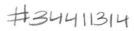

For
Roger and Annette Nicole

CONTENTS

PREFACE

I like the story (apocryphal? perhaps) of the open-air preacher who gathered a crowd by putting his hat on the sidewalk and circling around it, pointing to it and shouting, "It's alive!" When at last he picked the hat up, there under it was his Bible, and the livingness of the Word of God was his first theme as he unfolded the gospel of Jesus Christ.

This book aims to match that preacher's witness by exploring the true place, use, and benefit of the Bible—a topic on which I feel I can never say enough, let alone too much. Some of my material here has been printed before, but it seems to me that it all needs this present frame for its full thrust and force to appear.

Everything has been more or less rewritten for the present volume. For the record the chapters originated as follows: Chapter 1 began life as a mini-book titled in North America *Freedom and Authority* (1981) and in Britain *Freedom, Authority, and Scripture* (1982). Chapters 2 and 4 started in a book called *Beyond the Battle for the Bible* (1980; in Britain, *Under God's Word*). Chapter 3 is from a symposium edited by Harvie Conn, *Practical Theology and the Ministry of the Church* (1990). Chapter 5 expands what I wrote in *Inside the Sermon,* edited by Richard Allen Bodey. Chapter 6 develops some thoughts printed in *The Evangelical Catholic* (Jul./Aug. 1992). Occasional repetitions of detail from one chapter to another, which could not be eliminated without damaging the argument, will, I trust, be forgiven. "It is no trouble for me to write the same things to you again, and it is a safeguard for you" (Phil. 3:1).

May these pages bring readers closer to the experience of the psalmist who wrote:

> Oh, how I love your law!
>   I meditate on it all day long. . . .
> How sweet are your promises to my taste,
>   sweeter than honey to my mouth!
> I gain understanding from your precepts;
>   therefore I hate every wrong path.
>   (Psalm 119:97, 103-4)

1

GOD'S FREEDOM TRAIL
Authority and the Bible

"Authority" is a word that makes most people think of law and order, direction and restraint, command and control, dominance and submission, respect and obedience. How, I wonder, do you react to such ideas? Have they any place in your vision of the life that is good and sweet? If so, you are unusual. One tragedy of our time is that, having these associations, *authority* has become almost a dirty word in the Western world, while opposition to authority in schools, families, and society generally is cheerfully accepted as something that is at least harmless and perhaps rather fine.

How is it that so many today will tolerate expressions of defiance and disorder in society which a century ago would have been thought intolerable? Whence came the passionate permissiveness that has made a shambles of so many homes, schools, and individual lives? What goes on here? What is happening to us?

The Quest for Freedom

The answer to these questions is pinpointed by the fact that *freedom* is today almost a magic word. Since World War 2, when those who fought the dictators defined their war aims in terms of Four Freedoms—freedom from want, freedom from fear, freedom of speech, and freedom of religion—freedom in one form or another has been a worldwide passion, encouraged and catered to at every level. Therapists labor to induce freedom from inhibitions. *Playboy* carries the torch for sexual freedom ("free love" as it was once called, though there is little enough real love in *Playboy* sex). Campaigning politicians promise freedom from this or that social evil. Young nations seek freedom from the domination of overbearing neighbors. Artists pursue freedom from conventions of form and style which bound their predecessors.

Longings for freedom from restrictions, from the dead hand of the past, from disliked pressures, obligations, systems, and what not, are for many people the strongest of life's driving forces. Freedom—"getting out from under" as we say—has become modern man's obsession. And freedom is always seen as involving rejection of authority! Authority is equated with fixed limits, freedom with cutting loose from all that. Hence the crisis of authority which marks our time.

This way of conceiving freedom has its roots in philosophy: in dreams of the perfectibility of man, in Rousseau's idea that civilization squeezes you out of shape, in the educationists' fancy that inside each little demon is a little angel waiting to come out as soon as external pressures relax and interest is wooed. It is rooted in experience, too. Bad experiences of harsh and stifling authority at home, at school, in church, with the boss or the police, or elsewhere in the body politic have fueled fires of revolt. It is no wonder that rebels are hostile to what hurt them. The effect is that all forms of authority are seen as cell walls, which makes the quest for freedom feel like a Great Escape from some ideological prison-camp. Undisguised contempt for restrictions and directions, and truculent defiance which bucks all systems when it is not busy exploiting them, have become almost conventional, and anyone who respects authority stands out as odd. Modern man may claim to have come of age, but from this standpoint humanity seems to have regressed to adolescence. (Adolescents, of course, are always the first to insist on their own adulthood.) Surely today's rebellion against authority is a sign not of maturity but of its opposite. It is a form of folly, not of wisdom. It leads only to decadence and spoiled lives.

The truth, paradoxical yet inescapable, is this: there is no freedom apart from external authority. To say "I am my own authority, a law to myself" is to enslave myself to myself, which, as Seneca the Roman moralist said, is the worst bondage of all. Only as I bow to an authority which is not myself am I ever free. Let me explain.

What is authority? Authority is a relational word which signifies the right to rule. It is expressed in claims and is acknowledged by compliance and conformity. The word is used abstractly for the commanding quality which authoritative claims have, and also concretely for the source of such claims—"the authority" in each case. There are various sorts and sources of authority. Documents and authors are "the authorities" for scholars, statutes and past decisions for lawyers, parents for their young children, governors and law-enforcement personnel for us all. In the realms of belief, truth has authority; in realms of behavior, authority belongs to the moral law. In every situation it is wrong, and we know it is wrong, to disregard the form of authority that applies.

When historic Christianity receives the Bible as an absolute authority for creed and conduct, it does so on the basis that since God is a God of truth and righteousness, the instruction that he lays before us in writing must have the same qualities. The inerrancy debate about whether we should treat all Bible teaching as true and right is really about how far we can regard Scripture as authoritative.

Exercise of authority in its various spheres is not necessarily *authoritarian*. There is a crucial distinction here. Authoritarianism is authority corrupted, gone to seed. Authoritarianism appears when the submission that is demanded cannot be justified in terms of truth or morality, and actually harms those who submit. Nazism, Communism, Jim Jones's cult in Guyana, and David Koresh's Branch Davidians in Waco are examples. Any form of human authority can degenerate in this way. You have authoritarianism in the state when the regime uses power in an unprincipled way to maintain itself. You have it in churches and other religious groups when leaders claim control of their followers' consciences. You have it in academic work in high school, university, or seminary when you are required to agree with your professor rather than follow the evidence of truth for yourself. You have it in the

family when parents direct or restrict their children un-
reasonably. Unhappy experiences of authority are usually
experiences of degenerate authority, that is, of authoritarianism. That such experiences leave a bad taste and prompt
skepticism about authority in all its forms is sad but not
surprising.

Authoritarianism is evil, anti-social, anti-human, and ultimately anti-God (for self-deifying pride is at its heart),
and I have nothing to say in its favor. Legal and executive
power may be present to enforce authoritarian demands,
but nothing can make them respectable or praiseworthy.
Even when unprincipled requirements have legal right on
their side, as they sometimes do, they remain demands that
it was morally wrong to make.

When Christians affirm the authority of the Bible, meaning
that biblical teaching reveals God's will and is the instrument
of his rule over our lives, part of what they are claiming is
that Scripture sets before us the factual and moral nature of
things. God's law corresponds to created human nature, so
that in fulfilling his requirements we fulfill ourselves. The
gospel of Christ answers to actual human need, as glove
fits hand, so that all our responses to God work for our
good, and no touch of authoritarianism enters into his exercise of authority over us.

We talk about authority in order to sort out what factors
in a situation should determine our attitudes and actions.
The goal of such talk is to ensure that right decisions,
properly reached, do in fact get made. Whenever we credit
something with authority—a textbook, a ruling, a document, or whatever—we mean that in its own sphere it is
more or less decisive as a guide to what should be said or

done. When the risen Christ told his disciples, "All *authority* in heaven and on earth has been given to me" (Matt. 28:18), one implication was that all people everywhere should recognize his reign and treat his words as having decisive force for their lives. So he continued, "Therefore go and make disciples of all nations, . . . teaching them to obey everything I have commanded you" (vv. 19-20). When Christians debate whether Christ's authority attaches to what the church teaches or to what individual Christians think or to what the Bible says, they are not suggesting that these three never coincide or that two of them have no authority at all. What they are trying to decide is which of the three is *decisive*. The giving of decisive direction is what authority is all about.

Authority in human lives. Clearly, then, authority-principles will have formative and integrative effects on the communities and individuals that embrace them. By imposing a consistent method of decision-making, they dispel haphazardness and to that extent unify one's living. Those who acknowledge them as binding are left feeling that in trying to observe them you are doing what you should and that this makes life meaningful and worthwhile. To Christians, non-Christian authority-principles often seem ruinously wrong—the Marxist authority-principle, for instance, which requires everyone to work on a materialist basis for the socialized society that lies beyond the revolution; or the cultists' authority-principle that their leader (Sun Myung Moon or Jim Jones or David Koresh or whoever) should be listened to as God's infallible spokesman; or the authority-principle which prescribes the Buddhist, Hindu, or Islamic way of living. Yet it remains true that any fixed authority-principle gives life a goal and shape, a target, a program, and a yardstick of achievement, which it would not otherwise have. Only the Christian authority-principle leads to our chief end (glorifying and enjoying God, as the Westminster Shorter Catechism puts it). Yet just as drugs with lethal long-term effects, like heroin and cocaine, will for the moment make one feel brighter, so any authority-principle, however dubious, will in the short term make its devotees feel brighter—more integrated, more purposeful, more in shape—than they would feel with no such principle to hold their lives together. The one who knows no obligation to do anything lives the saddest, most aimless, most distracted life of all.

So the anti-authority syndrome now current in the West, leading as it does to lives of haphazard hedonism in which my feelings of like and dislike are the only authority I recognize, is a major human tragedy. We could hardly get further from the way we were meant to live.

Nor is the tragedy just personal. It touches society, too. History shows that many of the values basic to what we call civilization as opposed to savagery are biblical and Christian in origin. The world never knew them till it started living by the Christian authority-principle, and without that principle these values are unlikely to survive, at least in the decadent West as we know it. Take two examples.

First, we have inherited a belief in the dignity of womanhood and in the duty of men to honor and protect what Peter calls the weaker (more vulnerable, sooner hurt) sex (1 Pet. 3:7). This is founded in the scriptural teaching that both sexes bear God's image and share the same vocation as deputy governors of his world (Gen. 1:26-30), but it derives most directly, it would seem, from the unfailing courtesy, respect and goodwill toward women shown by Jesus (cf. Mark 7:25-30, 14:3-9; Luke 7:11-15, 36-50, 8:43-48, 10:38-42, 13:10-17, 23:27-31; John 4:7-26, 8:2-11, 11:20-44, 20:11-18; etc.). In the ancient Jewish and pagan world, as in Islam today, however important the woman's role as child-bearer, nurturer, and homemaker, it was taken for granted that she was the male's natural inferior as a human being. By changing that, Christianity did more to raise women's status than any other movement in history. When women's rights advocates censure biblical Christians for their doubts as to whether the fulfilling by women of historic male-leadership roles in church and state is pleasing to God, they usually forget that the starting point of their own arguments (the equal dignity of man and woman) is itself a Christian insight which can only be expected to fade when the authority of Christian truth is denied. It will be a small gain for women to have achieved professional interchange-ability with men if meantime men lapse into thinking that the height of masculinity is to treat women as playthings, each one fair game for male marauders.

Scripture knows the world of lust well (cf. Gen. 34, 35:22; 2 Sam. 11, 13) and seeks to wean us from it (Matt. 5:27-30; 1 Cor. 6:9-10; Gal. 5:19-21; Col. 3:5; 1 Thess. 4:3-6; etc.). But any generation that devalues Scripture may be expected to revert to living on that level. Indeed, we see it happening already. The *Playboy* philosophy, with the rest of the pattern of decline which Paul luridly pictures in Romans 1:21-32, Ephesians 4:18-19 and Colossians 3:5-8, is more familiar and socially acceptable today than it has been for centuries and looks like becoming yet more so in this era of supposedly "safe sex."

Second, we have inherited a belief in the sanctity of human life. This reflects the biblical insistence that we honor God by protecting and preserving the life he gives to us his image-bearers and that we dishonor him if we snuff that life out (save in judicial execution and war, which Scripture sees as special cases: cf. Gen. 9:6; Exod. 20:13 with 21:12-17; Rom. 13:4; Josh. 8:1-29; Judg. 15:14-19; etc.). Paganism, by contrast, has always held life to be cheap. Pagan philosophers, ancient and modern, have advocated suicide. Pagan communities, ancient and modern, have regularly placed babies out of doors to die. The Romans enjoyed watching gladiators kill each other and seeing Christians chewed up by lions. Widows in India were traditionally burned on their husbands' funeral pyres. Other twentieth-century pagans besides the Nazis, notably in Africa, Russia, Bosnia, and Cambodia, have practiced forms of genocide. Current arguments for abortion on demand and euthanasia by agreement show that some among us have already gone back to paganism at this point, and there is really no reason to expect that life will continue to be held sacred when the Bible is no longer revered. Pragmatic arguments for quietly killing those who can make no useful contribution to society, as the Nazis quietly killed off the mentally disabled, are at times obvious and appealing and only Scripture has ever given any communities anywhere motives for protecting the weak and helpless. Take away Scripture, and there is no telling where neo-pagan pragmatism will stop.

Today's drift from the authority of Christian truth—

indeed from acknowledging any external authority at all—is producing disintegrated and distracted individuals and a disordered and anarchic society. And it will continue to do so, with domestic, political, and economic consequences that can hardly be happy. Can the decline be arrested? Unfortunately, great numbers in our churches have so lost touch with the Christian authority-principle that even when they see which way things are going (which they often do not), they can do nothing to stop the rot. Whether the forces of biblical faithfulness can reverse the steady secularizing of the West is something only time will show. The sole certainty is that apart from biblical faithfulness such a reversal is not possible. A church in which scriptural teaching is no longer authoritative is already going with the world and has no ground on which to stand against it. If today's trend cannot be reversed, then the outlook for tomorrow's world is bleak indeed.

Such is the position regarding authority. Now we must discuss freedom.

What is freedom? Freedom, as was said, has become a word to conjure with. It is modern man's way to treat freedom as the supreme value in life. Everyone wants more freedom than he or she has, and the quick way to get a following is to lay claim to a formula whereby freedom may be increased. It makes Westerners feel good to see themselves as the "free world," just as it must have made the late Bertrand Russell feel good to announce his anti-Christianity in an essay entitled "A Free Man's Worship." Politicians, lawyers, educationists, and social planners, if asked in public what they are after, will certainly reply in terms of maximizing personal freedom. Many hail today's permissiveness as a social virtue because it gives freedom for deviant behavior which less tolerant ages would not have countenanced. "Liberty-equality-fraternity" was the war cry of the French Revolution, and the testimony of liberation-movements, literature, pop songs and political rhetoric all over the world is that liberty is no less vehemently sought today than it was in eighteenth-century France.

But what *is* liberty? Under what circumstances are we genuinely free? Ask this question, and the solid-looking front of freedom seekers breaks up at once. There is no agreement on the answer.

Basically there are two ways of conceiving freedom, and we have pointed to the first already. It is to view freedom as secular, external and this-worldly. It is essentially a matter of breaking bonds and abolishing restrictions and hardships. It seeks freedom *from* or freedom *not to*. Those who think thus of freedom have different ways of pursuing it. Some break out and, as they say, act out. These are the revolutionaries, social, moral, political and aesthetic, who constantly strive to stymie and overthrow "the system." Others drop out. These are the 1960s-style hippies, the counter-culturalists, those who hole up in rural communes and farms, do their own thing and never mind what the rest of the world is up to as long as they are left alone. Still others throw out. In the name of humanism these jettison Christianity with its supposedly dehumanizing restraints on conduct. Such also are those who seek to advance women's liberation by decrying the leadership role of men. The idea common to all these endeavors is that you gain freedom by negating something else.

The results are unimpressive. Revolutions turn out to be an exchange of one tyranny for another. Hippy-ness is found to be no passport to happiness. The self-styled "free-thinker" spends his strength denying what his parents or some other authority-figure once tried to teach him, and he never gets beyond it. Women challenging exclusive male leadership end up mannish and loud. Is any of this recognizable as the freedom for which we all inwardly long? The idea that freedom is what you have when you have thrown off all that represses or constrains you is a false trail which leads nowhere save to puzzlement and disillusioned bitterness.

The second approach to freedom is distinctively Christian. It is evangelical, personal, and positive. It defines freedom persuasively, that is, in terms which (so it urges) all should recognize as expressing what they are really after. These terms relate not to externals, which vary from age to age and person to person, but to the unchanging realities of the inner life. This definition starts with freedom *from* and freedom *not to*—in this case, freedom from the guilt and power of sin, and freedom not to be dominated by tyrannical self will—but it centers on freedom *for*: freedom for God and godliness, freedom to love and serve one's Maker and fellow-creatures, freedom for the joy, hope and contentment which God gives to sinners who believe in Christ. The essence of freedom (so the claim runs) lies in these inward qualities of heart, of which modern secular man knows nothing.

This approach sees freedom as the inner state of all who are fulfilling the potential of their own created nature by worshiping and serving their Savior-God from the heart. Their freedom is freedom not to do wrong, but to do right; not to break the moral law, but to keep it; not to forget God, but to cleave to him every moment, in every endeavor and relationship; not to abuse and exploit others, but to lay down one's life for them (cf. John 15:12-13; 1 John 3:16). Freedom for such free service and self-giving is beyond the capacity, even the comprehension, of fallen human nature. At first sight few can recognize it as freedom at all. Though it is really the way of life for which we were made, it so negates the self-absorbed lifestyle which we all instinctively choose that it seems to us anti-human and frightens us off. In fact, the only way anyone comes to know it at all is as the gift of the risen Christ, who affirms his penitent disciples in their self-denial and imparts his life to us as we give away our own.

One aspect of this freedom is *integrity*, that simplicity and purity of heart which, as Kierkegaard analyzed it, consists in willing one thing, namely the will and glory of God, so that one's motives are freed from the taint of self-regard. A second aspect is *spontaneity*. Unlike the rule-ridden Pharisees, whom Jesus pictured living (as it were) by numbers, the free person in Christ invests creative enterprise and resourcefulness in the task of pleasing and praising God and doing good to one's fellows. Where the Pharisee's concern is simply to avoid doing wrong, the free person seeks to make the most and best of every situation, thus becoming lively and sometimes breathtaking company. A final aspect is *contentment*, the fruit of God's gift of a joy within that increases all life's pleasures, stays with one whatever is present or lacking in one's outward circumstances, and enables one to accept without bitterness the most acute forms of suffering and pain. In short, the real Christian—for that is the person I am describing—is free for holiness, humanness and happiness—a freedom which surely merits its name.

Where does this freedom come from? Jesus Christ, the one perfectly free man that history has seen, is its source as well as its model. He himself said, "If the Son sets you free, you will be free indeed" (John 8:36; for biblical development of the thought see Rom. 6:1-7; and Gal. 4:21-6:10). The exchange from which this promise comes is worth noting. Jesus had said: "If you hold to my teaching . . . the truth will set you free" (John 8:31, 32). His Jewish hearers, bridling, had protested (with pathetic unrealism, in view of the Roman occupation), "We . . . have never been slaves of anyone" (John 8:33). Their protest showed them to be thinking of freedom in the purely external terms whose inadequacy we noted. But Jesus replied that he was talking of real freedom, freedom by comparison with which mere external non-servitude is not freedom at all. The real freedom is freedom from sin, which brings with it a place in God's family, which is the place of permanent external security. Jesus tells them that only those whom he himself has freed, as they have entrusted themselves to him, are free in this full sense. If you read the whole passage (John 8:31-36) you will see this at once.

Jesus did not say, nor do I, that freedom from external pressure is not worth seeking or should not actually be sought by those for whom true freedom has become a reality. That is a different issue. My point, rather, is that while enjoyment of external freedom does not guarantee a free heart, the freedom that Christ gives can be enjoyed—praise God!—whatever external pressures there may be.

Freedom, authority, and Scripture. It must be plain that the second view of freedom is the profounder of the two, and since this freedom is bound up with personal salvation, social usefulness, and the praise of God together, we should want to see everyone's feet set on the road to it. But that road takes the form of accepting authority—the authority of God the Creator, who designed and sustains our human nature and alone can tell us what best to do with it; the authority of Jesus Christ, God incarnate, the risen, reigning Son of God to whom all authority is given, who frees and keeps free those who continue in his word; the authority of Holy Scripture, which, as we shall see, is not just a witness to Christ's universal reign but is actually the instrument of it so far as humankind are concerned; and the authority of the Holy Spirit, who so opens and applies Scripture to our hearts that we discern Christ's will and are enabled to do it.

We saw earlier that accepting some external authority-principle is the precondition of order, integration, and stable purpose in one's life. What I am saying now is that the only authority-principle which imparts these blessings in a way that brings final satisfaction and salvation is the personal divine authority of "the man Christ Jesus" (1 Tim. 2:5), mediated by the Holy Spirit in and through the Bible. An ancient prayer addresses God as the one "whom to serve is to be free" ("whose service is perfect freedom," as the Anglican Prayer Book renders it). That is the truth we must face. We cannot have the freedom we want until we receive it on God's terms, that is, by giving up our rebellious independence and letting God be God to us. Real freedom is only ever found under authority—God's authority in Christ, authority which reaches us via God's written Word.

Once our society knew this well, but for a century now the Bible has been so much in eclipse, even in the churches, that the formula may well strike some as novel and others as incredible, because of the high view of Scripture which it implies. So far from being novel, however, that high view is authentic Christianity, and so far from being incredible it has as strong a claim on our acceptance as has any Christian truth. To show this is my next task.

Authority and Scripture

Built into Christianity is a principle of authority. This is because Christianity is revealed religion. It claims that God our Creator has acted to make known his mind and will, and therefore his revelation has authority for our lives. Biblical religion is marked by certainty about beliefs and duties. The diffidence and indefiniteness of conviction which thinks of itself as becoming humility has no place or warrant in Scripture, where humility begins with taking God's word about things. All through the Bible God's servants appear as folk who know what God has told them and are living by that knowledge. This is true of patriarchs, prophets, psalmists, apostles, other lesser lights and supremely of the Lord Jesus Christ himself.

Certainty and authority. Focus on Christ for a moment. He was the Son of God incarnate and as such had no will of his own. It was his nature, as well as his duty and delight, to do his Father's will in everything. He is on record as having said, "I do nothing on my own but speak just what the Father has taught me. . . . I always do what pleases him" (John 8:28-29; cf. 4:34, 5:30, 6:38, 8:26, 12:49-50, 14:31, 17:4). Jesus knew that his authority as his Father's messianic agent depended on his remaining subject to the Father in this way (he commended the Roman centurion for seeing that, Matt. 8:10 ff.).

That he was in his Father's will was to him a source of tremendous strength, as became very plain in the last week of his earthly life. One day he rode into Jerusalem at the head of a cheering crowd, like a king coming to be crowned. The next day, alone, he went through the temple like a hurricane, wrecking the bazaar in the Court of Gentiles, kicking out the stallholders, upsetting the bankers' desks and dazzling onlookers by the fury with which he denounced the business routines he had thus disrupted. The authorities huddled. Two big demonstrations in two days! What for? And what next? The day after, "while Jesus was walking in the temple courts, the chief priests, the teachers of the law and the elders came to him. 'By what authority are you doing these things?' they asked" (Mark 11:27-28). Jesus replied that his authority, like John's baptism, was from God. He was doing his Father's will and knew it, as he showed again two days later in Gethsemane ("not as I will, but as you will. . . . Your will be done. . . . It must happen in this way," Matt. 26:39, 42, 54). His Father's will was the constant control of his life.

Jesus was divine. The rest of us are not. So it might be expected that his followers would be less certain about God's mind and will than he was. In the New Testament, however, that is not so, whatever may be true of some Christians today. "Know" is a New Testament keyword, "we know" a New Testament refrain. These writers claim that Christians know God, his work, his will and his ways, because they have received revelation from him. They tell us that God's self-revelation has taken the form not only of action but also of instruction. God, so they say, has spoken in and through what Jesus said (Heb. 1:1-2 with 2:3). He has made known to apostles and prophets the secret of his eternal plan (Eph. 1:9-10, 3:3-11; cf. Rom. 16:25-26; 1 Cor. 2:6-11). Apostolic preachers relay his message "not in words taught . . . by human wisdom but in words taught by the Spirit" (1 Cor. 2:13). We receive this as "sound doctrine" (2 Tim. 4:3; Tit. 1:9, 2:1), "the truth" (2 Thess. 2:10, 12, 13, etc.), "the word of God" (1 Thess. 2:13, etc.) and thus gain sure and certain knowledge of God's mind. Modern theology will oppose the authority of Christ to that of Scripture, but in the New Testament bowing to Christ's lordship and believing God-taught doctrine entail each other.

Believing and obedience. Believing must lead to obedience. Christians have constantly been in trouble for defying human authorities and challenging consensuses. Peter would not stop evangelizing when told to (Acts 4:19-20, 5:27 ff.) and was in and out of prison as a result. Christians risked persecution in the early days by refusing the formalities of Roman state religion, just as latter-day African Christians have courted martyrdom by rejecting tribal rites. Athanasius sentenced himself to exile by standing against the Arian world. Luther jeopardized his life by refusing to recant at Worms. Christians today make themselves unpopular and forfeit various forms of advancement by opposing such social realities as the pornography trade and such social conveniences as abortion on demand. These are samples of the costly nonconformity that Christians have practiced down the ages.

Why do they behave so awkwardly? Because, standing under God's authority, they are sure that his revelation requires them to act as they do at whatever personal cost. Luther said at Worms, "My conscience is captive to the Word of God; to go against conscience is neither right nor safe; here I stand, there is nothing else I can do; God help me; amen." The privilege of knowing God's truth with certainty and precision carries with it the responsibility of obeying that truth with equal precision. Christianity is no armchair faith, but a call to action.

The problem of authority. But here a difficulty arises: whose version of revealed truth should be accepted? Imagine the perplexity of the Galatian Christians the day they first had read to them the blistering sentences in which Paul goes after some who "are trying to pervert the gospel of Christ" (Gal. 1:7). "As for those agitators, I wish they would go the whole way and emasculate themselves!" (Gal. 5:12). Imagine, too, how the Colossian Christians must have gulped when they first heard the words of Paul (whom they had never met) cutting down the teacher who was delighting in "false humility and the worship of angels" and who was puffed up "with idle notions" (Col. 2:18). In each case Paul was squelching respected men whose teaching on faith and duty had hitherto been treated as true. Whom should the believers then follow? Paul? Or their local pundits? And on what principle should they decide?

This problem is still with us. Roman Catholics, for example, say that Christians should treat the Pope as chief pastor of all Christendom and that his *ex cathedra* pronouncements, like those of councils, are infallible. They say that Christians should pray to Mary and see the eucharist as in some sense the church's sacrifice for its sins. With this Protestants disagree. Radicals deny Jesus' personal deity, objective sin-bearing, bodily resurrection and personal return. With this both Protestants and Catholics disagree. What should the plain Christian do when he or she finds fellow-believers at odds about the truth and will of God, some saying one thing, some another? What procedure should he follow in order to determine his own belief and behavior? There are just three options.

1. The church as authority. The Christian may treat the consensus of the church as decisive, making ecclesiastical tradition and conviction the authoritative guide to the authoritative will of God. This is what the Roman Catholic and Eastern Orthodox churches, with some Anglicans, tell us we should do. The implications of this rule of procedure will vary for individuals according to what they mean by "church" (church of Rome, early church, their own denomination, or whatever), but the principle is clear. You should approach the Bible as a product of the church and identify mainstream church teaching with the biblical faith. You should study Scripture by the light of that teaching and make Scripture fit in with it. Where the church has not pronounced, you may freely speculate. But you should take as from God all the definite instruction that the church gives. What the church says, God says. Therefore, the Holy Spirit's first step in teaching us is to make us docile under church authority.

2. *The individual as authority.* The Christian may treat his own ideas as decisive, whatever dissent from the Bible and the historic church that may involve. On this view, Scripture and church teaching are essentially resource material to help us make up our own minds. Both should be known. But neither need be endorsed, for neither is infallible and both include chaff as well as wheat. The theologies found in Scripture and Christian history are uneven attempts to verbalize a religious awareness in such terms as different cultures provided, and each is a mixture of facts and fancies, insights and mistakes. Our task is to sort out what seems lastingly valid and express that in contemporary terms. The principle is that what our own spirit says—that is, our reason, conscience and imagination—God says. The Holy Spirit's work is to sensitize our spirit to discern God's message to us in this way.

3. *The Bible as authority.* The Christian may treat Holy Scripture as decisive, according to the dictum of the Westminster Confession: "The supreme judge by which all controversies of religion are to be determined, and all decrees of councils, opinions of ancient writers, doctrines of men, and private spirits, are to be examined, and in whose sentence we are to rest, can be no other but the Holy Spirit speaking in the Scripture" (I, x). One who takes this line departs from the second view by receiving the Bible as God's authoritative instruction for all time and from the first view by subjecting the church's teaching and interpre-

tations to the judgment of the Bible itself as a self-interpreting whole. This person will look to the Holy Spirit who gave Scripture to authenticate its contents to God's people as God's truth, and to show them how it applies to their lives (cf. 1 John 2:20-27). This person's constant aim will be to have Scripture judge and correct all human ideas, including his or her own. This person will value the church's doctrinal and expository heritage very highly, but not give it the last word. The heart echoes Augustine's breathtaking utterance to God: "What your Scripture says, you say," and so he or she views the Spirit's teaching role as one first and foremost of keeping minds attuned to Scripture, the divine textbook.

To illustrate how these alternatives might work, let us imagine a debate about abortion on demand. An adherent of the first approach (call him a *traditionalist* or an *ecclesiasticist*) would oppose the practice because the church has always forbidden it. An adherent of the third approach (call her a *biblicist* or an *evangelical*) would oppose the practice because Scripture, understood in its own terms, forbids killing people and will not let us see the fetus as anything less than a person heading for a viable life. The adherent of the second approach (call him a *subjectivist* or a *relativist*) might well dismiss the biblical view of the fetus as unscientific, and regard prohibitions based on it as groundless and inappropriate. He might defend abortion on demand as compassionate to women, urging that unwanted babies are a bad thing and that modern medical technology makes the operation pretty safe. Each method challenges and points away from the other two, even when, as in the case of the first and second, the results of following them coincide.

Between these alternative methods of determining God's will, you and I must choose. They are not compatible, even when on particular points all three yield coinciding convictions. The first and the third, which both view Scripture as revealed truth that abides, are closer to each other than either is to the second, which treats biblical thought as a transient cultural product. Yet the gap between these two is wide, as the historic tension between Roman Catholicism and evangelical Protestantism shows. Individuals may and do oscillate inconsistently between the three alternatives, but as we noted a moment ago, each in itself excludes the other two.

Which method, then, is right? Which is authentically Christian? Which squares with the teaching and purpose of Christ and his apostles? Which would Jesus and Paul and John and Peter approve, were they back with us today to guide us? I think the answer is plain.

Christ's view of authority. Take Jesus first. There is no good reason to doubt the authenticity of what the gospels say of him. They were evidently written in good faith and with great care by knowledgeable persons (cf. Luke 1:1-4; John 19:35, 21:24). They were composed at a time when Jesus was still remembered, and misstatements about him could be identified. They were accepted everywhere, it seems, as soon as they were known, though the early Christians as a body were not credulous and detected spurious gospels with skill. The consensus of the centuries has been that these four portraits of Jesus have a ring of truth. While it is easy to believe that so awesome and unconventional a figure as Jesus, with his divine self-awareness and claims, would be well remembered—would, indeed, prove unforgettable—it is not credible that he should have been made up. It is safe to say that not even Shakespeare, who created Lear, Hamlet and Falstaff, could have invented Jesus Christ! Granted, individual scholars doubt various gospel facts and details, but in every field of study there is always some scholar ready to query what his peers affirm, and anyone who reflects on the probabilities of the case will soon see that such paradoxical doubts should not weigh heavily with straightforward people. We may be confident, then, that in reading the gospels we meet the real Jesus. And the gospels set before us the following facts about what Jesus thought and taught.

1. *Jesus' authority.* Fully aware of his unique identity as Son of the Father, Jesus claimed absolute personal authority in all his teaching: "It was said. . . . But I tell you" (Matt. 5:21-22); "He taught as one who had authority, and not as their teachers of the law" (Matt. 7:29); "Heaven and earth will pass away, but my words will never pass away" (Mark 13:31). He said that our destiny depends on whether, having heard his words, we heed them or not: "There is a judge for the one who rejects me and does not accept my words; that very word which I spoke will condemn him at the last day. For I did not speak of my own accord, but the Father who sent me commanded me what to say and how to say it. . . . So whatever I say is just what the Father has told me to say" (John 12:48-50; see also Matt. 7:24-27; Luke 6:47-49).

2. *Old Testament authority.* Fully conscious of his own divine identity, Jesus taught the absolute divine authority of the Jewish Scriptures. Some 200 references in the gospels

combine to make his view of our Old Testament crystal clear. He saw the books as having both human authors and a divine author, so that, for example, commands which Moses presents as the word of God are indeed such (Mark 7:8-13) and an expository comment in Genesis 2:24 can be quoted as what "the Creator . . . said" (Matt. 19:4-5). As God's word, disclosing his truth, purpose, and command, Scripture has abiding authority (John 10:35; Matt. 5:18-20).

It is striking to see how Jesus, while setting his personal authority against that of earlier rabbinic interpreters (which is what he was doing when he contrasted what "was said" with what "I tell you"), always bowed and taught others to bow to Scripture as such. He gave the key to his whole ministry when he said, "Do not think that I have come to abolish the Law or the Prophets; I have not come to abolish them but to fulfill them" (Matt. 5:17), that is, to be fully subject to them as they applied to him. From Scripture he resolved questions of doctrine (the resurrection, Mark 12:24-27; the intended permanence of marriage, Matt. 19:5-6) and ethics (the rightness of letting need override Sabbath restrictions, Matt. 12:2-8; the wrongness of *corban* casuistry as a cop-out from the obligations of the fifth commandment, Mark 7:10-13). By Scripture he justified the acts of his ministry (cleansing the temple, Mark 11:15-17). By it he discerned his personal calling to be the Servant-Messiah who must enter upon his reign by the path of death and resurrection (Matt. 26:53-56; Mark 12:10-11, 14:21; Luke 18:31 ff., 22:37, 24:25 ff., 44 ff.; cf. Matt. 4:4, 7, 10). His resurrection would be his vindication, the Father's seal of approval set publicly on all the Son had said and done—including what he said about Scripture and his going to Jerusalem to die in obedience to Scripture. It is surely significant that on the resurrection day he was found with two groups of disciples explaining how Scripture had been fulfilled in his dying and rising to reign (Luke 24:25 ff., 46 ff.).

3. *New Testament authority.* Jesus conferred his own authority on the apostles to go out in his name as his witnesses and spokesmen. In appointing them his messengers, Jesus promised them the Spirit to enable them to fulfill their task (Mark 13:11; Luke 24:47 ff.; John 14:25-26, 15:26-27, 16:7-15, 20:21-23; Acts 1:8), and he prayed for his people, present and future, in just two categories: first, the apostles; second, "those who will believe in me through their message" (John 17:20). Thus, he showed that the apostles' witness to Christ would be both the norm and the means of all other Christians' faith to the end of time. What we call the New Testament is a set of books which embody that witness, and thus make it permanently and universally available. To find in John 17:20 a virtual promise of the New Testament, as Christian teachers have done for centuries, is perfectly natural.

Apostolic authority. The rest of the New Testament, accompanying the gospels—a history book (Acts), twenty-one pastoral letters, and a book that begins with seven further letters and then becomes an apocalypse—is as we would expect in light of these facts. On one hand, the apostles are conscious of their role as Christ's commissioned representatives and of the God-givenness and divine authority of their teaching. This is especially clear in Paul and John, who both addressed situations where their authority had been challenged.

In 1 Corinthians 2:12-13 Paul claims both inward illumination and verbal inspiration for his message. In 1 Corinthians 14:36-38 and 2 Thessalonians 3:6-12 he insists that his directives must be taken as commands of the Lord whom he represents. In Galatians 1:8-9, he solemnly curses anyone who brings a different message from his own.

John calmly but breathtakingly states in black and white that, "We [apostolic witnesses] are from God, and whoever knows God listens to us; but whoever is not from God does not listen to us. This is how we recognize the Spirit of truth and the spirit of falsehood" (1 John 4:6).

Bolder authority-claims could hardly be made. The apostles are no less sure than were the Old Testament prophets that their message was from God.

But, on the other hand, with equal emphasis they claim the Jewish Scriptures as divine instruction for Christians, prophetically proclaiming Christ, the gospel and the realities of discipleship to the church. "The holy Scriptures . . . are able to make you wise for salvation through faith in Christ Jesus. All Scripture is God-breathed and is useful for teaching, rebuking, correcting and training in righteousness, so that the man of God may be thoroughly equipped for every good work" (2 Tim. 3:15-17). Of what he calls "the prophetic writings" or "the oracles of God" Paul declares, "Everything that was written in the past was written to teach us, so that through endurance and the encouragement of the Scriptures we [Christians] might have hope" (Rom. 15:4; cf. 1 Cor. 10:11). Old Testament passages are quoted as God's speech in Acts (4:25; 28:25) and Hebrews (3:7, 10:15), and Paul's phrases "the Scripture says to Pharaoh" (Rom. 9:17) and "the Scripture foresaw . . . and announced the gospel in advance to Abraham" (Gal. 3:8) show how completely he himself equated Scripture with God speaking—we might even say, God preaching. That the Jewish Scriptures have God's plan concerning Christ as their main subject is everywhere taken for granted. In Hebrews, the deity, manhood and mediation of Christ are the doctrinal themes, and every point up to the start of chapter 13 is made by expounding and applying the Old Testament. The New Testament view of the Old is thus consistent and clear.

So the Jewish Scriptures were held to be authoritative, God-given witness to Christ, just as apostolic preaching was. In both cases the authority was seen not as human, the relative yet uneven authority of insight and expertise, but as divine, the absolute, oracular authority of God telling us truth about his work and his will, and about the worship and obedience that we owe him. Not all that was said, whether by the Old Testament or by the apostles, was equally important, but all was part of the rule of faith and life inasmuch as it came from God.

Since Jewish Scripture and apostolic preaching were on a par, it was as natural as it was momentous that Peter, having reminded his readers that Old Testament Scripture came as "men . . . were carried along by the Holy Spirit" (2 Pet. 1:21), should bracket Paul's sermons on paper (which is what his letters were) with "the other scriptures" (3:16) and admonish his readers to heed both and not mishandle either. Here the Christian authority-principle at last becomes explicit: the Old Testament read in conjunction with the apostolic presentation of Christ or, putting it the other way around, the apostolic presentation of Christ conjoined with the Old Testament is the rule of faith for Jesus' disciples. God now teaches, reproves, corrects and instructs in and by what is written in the two Testaments together.

Despite the newness of the New Testament, the principle that the written Word of God must shape faith and life was old. The basis of Old Testament religion was that God has spoken in human language and has caused his teaching to be recorded for permanence, and that the way to please him is to go by the book. All Jesus' teaching and ministry assumed this. What follows, then? Should we say that he founded Christianity on a fallacy? Or should we not rather say that by endorsing this basic Jewish tenet he showed that it was true?

Here we reach a crucial point for our own faith. So far we have been appealing to the Bible simply as a good historical source, from which we may learn with certainty what the founders of Christianity taught. But if Jesus was God incarnate and spoke with personal divine authority, and if by sending the Spirit he really enabled his apostles to speak God's word with total consistency, it follows that both Testaments (that which his gift of the Spirit produced as well as that which he knew and authenticated) ought to be received as "the very words of God" and as "God-breathed and . . . useful . . . so that the man of God may be thoroughly equipped" (Rom. 3:2; 2 Tim. 3:16-17). Only as we seek to believe and do what the two Testaments, taken together, teach have we the full right to call ourselves Jesus' disciples. "Why do you call me, 'Lord, Lord,' and do not do what I say?" (Luke 6:46). Scripture comes to us, as it were, from Jesus' hand, and its authority and his are so interlocked as to be one.

Bowing to the living Lord entails submitting mind and heart to the written Word. Disciples individually and churches corporately stand under the authority of Scripture because they stand under the lordship of Christ, who rules by Scripture. This is not bibliolatry but Christianity in its most authentic form.

Biblical authority. So we learn from Christ to learn from Scripture as God's authoritative Word. We may spell out the theology of that lesson as follows.

1. The Creator communicates. God made us in his image, rational and responsive, so that he and we might live in fellowship. To this end, he makes himself known to us. He enters into communication with a view to communion. Always he has caused his works of creation and providence to mediate some sense of his reality, righteousness, and glory to all who are alive in his world, however little they welcome this. "Since the creation of the world God's invisible qualities—his eternal power and divine nature— have been clearly seen, being understood from what has been made" (Rom. 1:20; cf. 1:32; 2:14 ff.; Acts 14:16-17; Ps. 19:1 ff.). Moreover, God speaks in ordinary human words, using his own gift of language to tell us about himself. We read that verbal revelation began in Eden before man fell (Gen. 2:16-17) and that all that God has made known for salvation was first revealed verbally to and through patriarchs, prophets, apostles, and Jesus Christ, whereupon it was embodied in the books that make up our Bible (Rom. 15:4; Gal. 3:8; Eph. 3:4 ff.; Heb. 2:3; 1 Pet. 1:10 ff.).

2. God reveals salvation. The general formula here is that God reveals himself so that humankind may know him.

The specific formula is that God reveals himself as Savior so that sinners may know him savingly. Here are four connected strands of divine activity:

First and most basic was God's historical self-disclosure by redemptive deeds prefaced and followed by explanatory words, a sequence of acts that began with the patriarchs and the exodus and reached its climax in the messianic ministry, atoning death, and triumphant resurrection of Jesus, whereby, as Zechariah sang, God "raised up a horn of salvation for us in the house of his servant David" (Luke 1:69). The good news of these acts is the *gospel*.

Second and distinct from this was God's work of inspiring expository, celebratory and applicatory records of his words and deeds, so that all might know what he had done and would do, and what their response should be. The collection of these records is the *Bible*.

The third strand in God's revelatory work is his providential action in bringing to each individual's notice what Holy Scripture has made public and permanently available. He does this through his messengers who spread the good news. The generic name for this activity, which includes all forms and modes of instruction and is meant to involve all God's people, is *preaching*.

Fourth and following on from the third is the giving of understanding so that those instructed believe the message and commit themselves to the Savior who is its subject. This inner enlightening is called *revelation* in Matthew 11:27, 16:17 and Galatians 1:16, but the usual name for it is *illumination*, according to the imagery of 2 Corinthians 4:6 and Ephesians 1:17-21.

All four modes of divine action—redemptive revelation in history, didactic revelation in Scripture, relayed revelation in the church's preaching and teaching, and illuminative revelation in the hearer's heart—are necessary if we are to know God as savior through Christ. The first two modes ceased in the first century A.D., but the third and fourth continue. The fourth is necessary because, although the Bible message authenticates itself as God's truth by the light and power that flow from it, fallen humans are unresponsive and indeed resistant to it, so that without illumination the gospel will only be doubted, devalued and finally ignored (Luke 14:15-24; 2 Cor. 4:3 ff.). God must enable us to see what he has revealed to the world in Jesus Christ, or we shall stay blind to it.

3. *God's Spirit teaches through Scripture.* The Spirit of Christ who indwells Christians never leads them to doubt, criticize, go beyond, or fall short of Bible teaching. Spirits which do that are not the Spirit of Christ (1 John 4:1-6). Rather, the Holy Spirit makes us appreciate the divine authority of Scripture, so that we accept its account of spiritual realities and live as it calls us to do. As the Spirit gave the Word by brooding over its human writers and leading the church to recognize their books as its canon for belief and behavior, so now he becomes the authoritative interpreter of Scripture as he shows us how biblical teaching bears on our living. To be sure, what Bible books meant as messages to their first readers can be gleaned from commentaries. But what they mean for our lives today is something we learn only as the Spirit stirs our insensitive consciences. Never does the Spirit draw us away from the written Word, any more than from the living Word. In-

stead, he keeps us in constant, conscious, contented submission to both together. He exerts his authority precisely by making real to us the divinity, Saviorhood, power, and presence of the Christ set forth in Scripture, and with that the personal authority of Christ over us *through* Scripture. This is what it means to be Spirit-taught and Spirit-led.

4. *Scripture promotes ethics.* Some fear that full acceptance of biblical authority must result in a legalistic lifestyle. The root of their fear seems to be a belief that God's law in Scripture really is a code of mechanical, impersonal do's and don'ts, in other words, that the Pharisees' view of the law was essentially right. But Jesus' scorching comments on the Pharisees showed that this view is wrong. The truth is that the moral teaching of Scripture focuses the ideal of creative goodness which Christ actually lived out. It requires us not just to stay within the limits of specific commands and prohibitions as if outward correctness was the essence of virtue and nothing more was required, but to stay within those limits so that we can make the best of every situation and relationship for the glory of God and the good of others. Law-keeping must be love in action. This is the one truth embedded in the otherwise false scheme of "situation ethics," which refuses to accept the law laid down in Scripture as the teaching of God. The ethical creativity which is always asking what is the best we can do is one dimension of that Christlike holiness to which we are called, and those who believe most strongly in the authority of Scripture should be manifesting more of this quality than anyone else.

5. *Scripture controls Christian consciences.* Consciences not governed by God's Word are to that extent not Christian.

"God alone is Lord of the conscience and hath left it free from the doctrines and commandments of men, which are, in any thing, contrary to his Word" says the Westminster Confession (XX, ii). One thinks again of Luther's statement at Worms: "My conscience is captive to the Word of God: to go against conscience is neither right nor safe." If conforming to ecclesiastical, governmental, marital, or parental demands involves action contrary to Scripture, God can only be served by nonconformity at that point. This may put us out of step with others and prove costly to us, but nothing less will please God. Conversely, when we find Scripture requiring of us goals and standards which are not the way of the world (going the second mile, turning the other cheek, loving our enemies) we may not excuse ourselves by reflecting that nobody else behaves like that. "Do not conform any longer to the pattern of this world," wrote Paul, "but be transformed by the renewing of your mind. Then you will be able to test and approve what God's will is—his good, pleasing and perfect will" (Rom. 12:2). "Test and approve" is one word in Greek, signifying the discernment of a consecrated conscience applying the generalities of God's Word to the specifics of one's personal life.

Scripture and freedom. We saw earlier that true freedom is only found under God's authority. What we are seeing now is that it is only found under the authority of Scripture, through which God's authority is mediated to all and Christ by his Spirit rules his people's lives. Biblical authority is often expounded in opposition to lax views of truth. Not so often, however, is it presented as the liberating, integrating, invigorating principle that it really is. The common idea is that unqualified confidence in the Bible leads to narrow-minded inhibitions and crippling restraints on what you may think and do. The truth is that such confidence produces liberated living—living, that is, which is free from uncertainty, doubt, and despair—living of a kind which otherwise is not found anywhere. The one who trusts the Bible knows what God did, does, and will do, what he commands and what he promises. With the Colossians, the Bible-believer understands "God's grace in all its truth" (Col. 1:6), for the Christ of Scripture has become the believer's Savior, master, and friend. Since Scripture shines as a lamp to his feet and a light for his path (Ps. 119:105), the believer can pick his way through the pitfalls of our spiritually benighted world without stumbling and travel through life with what the title of a famous old tract called "safety, certainty and enjoyment."

Such is the freedom (and the victory) found under the authority of the Bible. Such is the basic shape and style of the life in which the fullness of God's power comes to be known. And who can do without that? There are few aspects of the Christian message with which the church and the world need so urgently to be faced as the truth—the precious, stabilizing, enriching truth—of the full trustworthiness and divine authority of the written Word of God.

Authority and Inerrancy

Is our argument finished? Not quite. One matter still calls for discussion.

The fashion in scholarship. I said at the start that in the realm of belief, authority belongs to truth and truth only. I stick to that. I can make no sense—no reverent sense, anyway—of the idea, sometimes met, that God speaks his truth to us in and through false statements by biblical writers, any more than I can make moral sense of Plato's commendation of the useful lie. Accordingly, I have reasoned about the authority of Scripture on the assumption that it contains God-taught truth throughout.

But at this many skeptical eyebrows go up. For the past hundred years and more among Protestants most books published on the Bible, most teachers in most seminaries, and most clergy in most churches have told the world that scientific study of the Scriptures (called "critical" because it consciously evaluates its data) has made it impossible to believe all that the Bible says. Critical theories about the Bible have accumulated: for example, the critical theories of authorship, which view some books of both Testaments as spurious and so as spoofs; critical theories about composition, which see some of the historical matter in both Testaments as fanciful latter-day invention; and critical claims that Scripture is chock full of irreconcilable contradictions. The impact of theories has been to produce an atmosphere in which most ordinary people today seem convinced, on the say-so not just of unbelievers but of the Protestant academic establishment, that sensible persons must now treat the trustworthiness of the Bible as an exploded myth.

It should be added, to complete the picture, that whereas Roman Catholicism officially held to full biblical inerrancy till the second Vatican Council, its scholars have recently swallowed a great deal of Protestant skepticism. It thus looks as if the older belief will soon be a minority position in Catholicism too.

How should this state of affairs be viewed? I offer the following comments.

First, we should recognize the ingenuity of critical theories and the ability of their exponents. To think of these latter, as some have done, as if they were cretins and crooks, lacking academic ability and integrity just as they lack some elements of Christian orthodoxy, is a mistake. They have in fact been individuals of rare distinction, and the current dominance of their viewpoint is testimony to the persuasive skill with which they have expounded it.

Second, we should understand that the critical approach is nowadays an accepted convention of professional biblical scholarship. Sociologists of knowledge distinguish between *theories* and *paradigms,* defining the latter as the presuppositional frame of reference within which theories are formed. Whereas biblical infallibility was once a paradigm for Christian scholars in all fields, biblical fallibility is the accepted paradigm today.

I once heard a British university professor of theology tell a conference of his peers that New Testament studies are currently healthy, for everything held by anybody is being challenged by somebody. Modern academics, like ancient Athenians, enjoy having new theories to dissect, and it is understandable (if regrettable) that a biblical technician should treat a rank growth of critical opinions as a good sign. Then, too, many theologians today seem to feel that they owe it to their non-Christian peers in other disciplines to doubt as much as they can of their own Christianity and so escape the suspicion of being bigoted—a quixotic policy which seems as goofy as it does gratuitous. (Do Marxist academics behave like that?) But the fact remains that biblical skepticism is in fashion as a paradigm of scholarship. It is regarded as an academic virtue. Your scholarly credentials become suspect if you disclaim it, and many teachers make a point of pushing it down students' throats to deliver them from what is seen as naive credulity and the closed mind. Like other things taken for granted, it is not easily challenged. He who threatens a sacred cow finds great crowds threatening him and is made to feel very much the odd man out.

Third, we should note that biblical skepticism, even in small doses, has effects that reach further than career academics in their ivory towers sometimes see. In principle, it marks abandonment of the axiom that what Scripture says, God says. Once that happens—once, that is, you give up the New Testament view of biblical inspiration—there is no limit on how far you will go in rejecting or relativizing biblical assertions. There is no limit apart from your own arbitrary will. Protestantism's current confusion is largely due to the way its teachers have fanned out at this point, producing as many different sub-biblical theologies as there have been thinkers to devise them.

Fourth, we should realize that this whole development of biblical study, however dazzling in detail, was and is unnecessary. Biblical criticism developed in Germany had skepticism built into it from the start in the form of Kant's denial that God communicates verbally with man (a denial which strikes at the Bible's main claim and message), plus the eighteenth-century rationalist assumption that miracles do not happen. Naturally, the skepticism present in its premises comes out in its conclusions. But today, as in the past, a responsible biblical scholarship exists with the full truth of Scripture as its basic premise. It keeps its end up convincingly (so I judge) when interacting with critical opinion. It copes with the phenomena of Scripture, including the apparent discrepancies, at least as plausibly as does scholarship of the skeptical kind. The works of reference and resource which it produces bear comparison with any written from a rival standpoint. (Look, for instance, at the *New International* commentary series, and the various commentary series put out by InterVarsity Press, Word Books, Moody Press, and Broadman and Holman; also at *The New Bible Commentary, The New Dictionary of Theology, The New Bible Dictionary, The Evangelical Dictionary of Theology,* and *The New International Dictionary of New Testament Theology,* if you want to verify that.) While Bible-believing scholarship thus maintains itself, the claim that Holy Scripture can no longer be regarded as wholly trustworthy is plain nonsense.

Affirming inerrancy. A further point arises. It concerns the word *inerrancy,* which Protestants and Roman Catholics have been using for more than a century to denote the quality of entire trustworthiness which Bible-believers ascribe to the written Word. Those who hold themselves free to disbelieve details of what the Bible tells us naturally disclaim belief in inerrancy. Others, however, who claim to cleave to all that Scripture teaches, nonetheless object to the word and carefully avoid it when spelling out their faith in Scripture, as if they do not think it fits the facts. This is perplexing.

The fact is that these folks run scared. They are frightened of certain mental attitudes and stances with which they feel the word *inerrancy* is now inseparably linked and which in their view tend to obscure the Bible's main message and bar the way to the best in biblical scholarship. Specifically, they hear the inerrancy-claim as challenging all corners to find mistakes in Scripture if they can—which, so they think, is an improper diverting of interest from the great issues of the gospel to the minutiae of Bible harmony, and from believing proclamation to rationalistic apologetics. Also, they hear the inerrancy-claim as implying that the Bible can be proved true by secular inquiry and as centering attention on questions of its scientific and historical correctness. They think the claim leads to a sort of interpretation that overlooks the width of the cultural gap between Bible times and our own, and the extent to which our criteria of truth and accuracy fail to apply to biblical material. Because they wish to dissociate themselves from these tendencies, they decline to speak of inerrancy.

I sympathize. Yet I wonder if they have chosen the wisest and most fruitful course of action. I say this as one who over the years has moved in the opposite direction. Once I too avoided the word *inerrancy* as much as I could, partly because I had no wish myself to endorse the tendencies mentioned, and partly because the word has a negative form and I like to sound positive. But I find that nowadays I need the word. Verbal currency, as we know, can be devalued. Any word may have some of its meaning rubbed off, and this has happened to all my preferred terms for stating my belief about the Bible. I hear folk declare Scripture *inspired* and in the next breath say that it misleads from time to time. I hear them call it *infallible* and *authoritative*, and find they mean only that its impact on us and the commitment to which it leads us will keep us in God's grace, not that it is all true.

This is not enough for me. I want to safeguard the historic evangelical meaning of these three words and to make clear my intention, as a disciple of Jesus Christ, to receive as from the Father and the Son all that Scripture, when properly interpreted—that is, understood from within, in terms of its own frame of reference—proves to be affirming. So I assert inerrancy after all. I think this is a clarifying thing to do, since it shows what I mean when I call Scripture inspired, infallible, and authoritative. In an era of linguistic devaluation and double-talk we owe this kind of honesty to one another.

Assertors of inerrancy, however, need constantly to be making two points if misunderstandings are to be avoided. The first is negative, the second positive.

First, the assertion of inerrancy does not bear directly on the task of exegesis. Exegesis means drawing from each passage the meaning and message which it was written to convey to its writer's own first readers. The exegetical task is to read everything out of the text while taking care to read nothing into it. Biblical interpretation comprises exegesis, followed by a synthesis of findings within a biblical frame of reference, followed by application of the truths about God and man that have emerged to questions of faith and life today. Moreover, it must be done throughout in a way that can be justified from biblical data and is free from prejudices imported out of the thought-world of today's culture. Belief in inerrancy will affect the rigor with which one synthesizes and applies, but in exegesis the question is not yet one of truth, only one of meaning, and the assertion of inerrancy is not a shortcut to determining what texts mean. We can only do that by studying the flow of thought to which each text belongs. In this, inerrantists and noninerrantists are on exactly the same footing.

Second, the assertion of inerrancy bears directly on our theological method. What it says is that in formulating my theology I shall not consciously deny, disregard, or arbitrarily relativize anything that I find Bible writers teaching, nor cut the knot of any problem of Bible harmony, factual or theological, by assuming that the writers were not consistent with themselves or with each other. Instead, I shall labor to harmonize and integrate all that is taught (without remainder), to take it as from God (however little I may like it), and to seek actively to live by it (whatever change of my present beliefs and behavior-patterns it may require). This is what acceptance of the Bible as wholly God-given and totally true requires of us.

Following God's Freedom Trail

In Boston, Massachusetts, there is an official Freedom Trail, a tour of key sites connected with the War of Independence. Christianity knows another freedom trail, which the foregoing pages have sought to point out. The Boston freedom trail celebrates the gaining of political independence through fighting the British. The Christian freedom trail has to do with surrendering personal independence as one ceases to fight God. The point I have sought to make is that the freedom for which we were created is only enjoyed under the authority of God in Christ, and the only way we come under that authority and stay under it is by submitting in faith and obedience to what is in the Bible. The path to true personal freedom under God is acknowledgement of the authority of the Bible and its Christ. The gospel finds us rebels, guilty, lost and hopeless, and leads us for salvation to the feet of Christ, who teaches us to live by Scripture, in the power of the Holy Spirit.

The importance of recognizing biblical inerrancy as a fact of faith is that, on the one hand, it reminds us that all Scripture is instruction in one way or another from the God of truth. On the other hand, it commits us to consistency in believing, receiving, and obeying everything that it proves to say. The more completely heart and mind are controlled by Scripture, the fuller our freedom and the greater our joy. God's free servants know God and know about God. They observe God-taught standards and restraints in living and in relationships. They trust God's promises and in the power of Bible certainties live out their days in peace and hope. Modern man needs to hear more of this message of freedom from the church. The church needs to learn again how basic to that message is the truth of the inerrancy of Scripture, on which the fullness of biblical authority depends.

We have reached a place in the history of our culture where stable relationships based on respect, goodwill, fidelity, and service are breaking down, and alienation is becoming commonplace. Husbands and wives, parents and children, students and their instructors, employers and their employees, are increasingly estranged from each other in loneliness and hostility. A new and nasty feature of this eroding of relationships is that it is often justified in the

name of freedom, meaning the abandoning of commit-
ments, restrictions and restraints. Actually, the idea that
freedom requires uncommittedness or an adversary relationship toward other people is a sign of how far our society has drifted from its former understanding of what it
means to be truly human and (equally important) godly.
Our negative attitudes in relationships and our insistence
in doing our own thing, pursuing personal pleasure no
matter who gets hurt, show that we are not really free at
all. We are estranged not merely from men but also from
God and are in bondage to the grim perversion of nature
which the Bible calls sin and diagnoses as willed disregard
of God and his Word.

"When you were slaves to sin," wrote Paul to the Roman
Christians, "you were free from the control of righteousness. What benefit did you reap at that time from the
things you are now ashamed of? Those things result in
death! But now that you have been set free from sin and
have become slaves to God" (which is what becoming a
Christian means; when you put your trust in Jesus Christ
you become God's slave through repentance and are freed
from sin's dominion by regeneration), "the benefit you
reap leads to holiness, and the result is eternal life. For the
wages of sin is death, but the gift of God is eternal life in
Christ Jesus our Lord" (Rom. 6:20 ff.).

True freedom—freedom from blind-mindedness and sin,
freedom for God and righteousness—is found where Jesus
Christ is Lord in living personal fellowship. It is under the
authority of a fully trusted Bible, however, that Christ is
most fully known, and this God-given freedom most fully
enjoyed. Any degree of skepticism about the portrait of

Christ, the promises of God, the principles of godliness, and the power of the Holy Spirit, as biblically presented, has the effect of enslaving us to our own alternative ideas about these things, and thus we miss something of the freedom, joy, and vitality that the real Christ bestows. God is very patient and merciful, and I do not suggest that those who fall short here thereby forfeit all knowledge of Christ, though I recognize that when one sits loose to Scripture this may indeed happen. But I do maintain most emphatically that one cannot doubt the Bible without far-reaching loss, both of fullness of truth and of fullness of life. If therefore we have at heart spiritual renewal for society, for churches and for our own lives, we shall make much of the entire trustworthiness—that is, the inerrancy—of Holy Scripture as the inspired and liberating Word of God.

2

FORMED, DEFORMED, REFORMED
The Church and the Bible

"They lived happily ever after." So say fairy tales of imaginary married couples, and so wrote middle-aged Winston Churchill in the closing sentence of *My Early Life* about his own marriage with Clementine Hosier. I take him to have been telling the world two things. The first, which is there on the surface, is that they had become consciously inseparable, and the bond between them was growing stronger all the time. The second, which human nature makes certain though it was not stated, is that they had had ups and downs ("Christian rows," as a clergyman friend once put it), and would doubtless have more. But they had reached the point of knowing that their relationship would survive the arguments and not be destroyed by them. The fairy-tale phrase does not hint at this, nor at the inner complexity of the marriage relationship, from any standpoint at all; that knowledge is supplied only by experience.

Something similar is true of the relation between the

Bible and the church. The Bible is and always has been the book of the church, the source of its faith, thought, preaching, teaching, order, worship, praise, prayer, and song. The inseparability is conscious; the church always has been, and when in its senses has tried to show itself to be, the church of the book, learning its identity, calling, mission, knowledge of God, and knowledge of itself in and under God, from the pages of Holy Writ. Bunyan's pilgrim with his book in his hand could be a picture of the church no less than of the Christian. But this is not the whole story. The relation between Bible and the church has so varied in different periods and in different theologies that accusations of destroying it have often been heard within the church's own ranks, as in some places they are heard today. Also, though the relation may be simple and straightforward in idea, it regularly proves tense and complex in practice, because Bible and church are both intrinsically complex realities. Our first step in approaching our theme, therefore, had better be to warn ourselves against oversimplifying.

A Look at History

A glance at history gives perspective. The first major debate on Bible-church relations took place at the Reformation, when Roman and anti-Roman groups began to accuse each other of laying waste the church through misunderstanding Scripture. Up till then Christians had been taught to assume that the church's religion was identical with biblical faith, and any who did not agree were categorized as heretical monsters. The Reformers queried this identity at a deep level. They accused Rome of contradicting Scripture over the mediation of Christ; the work of the Spirit; the way of salvation; the method of grace; the meaning of justification and faith; the doctrine and use of the sacraments, especially the Lord's Supper; and the nature of the church itself. They also diagnosed the Roman appeal to tradition as binding and gagging the Bible so that it could not speak and be heard. For saying this the Reformers were, to be sure, categorized as heretical monsters, but they made their point at least to this extent: They compelled Rome to argue for her position and to recognize that it could no longer be taken for granted.

In that debate the main issues were the *extent, clarity,* and *sufficiency* of Scripture. On the first issue Rome said: The canon of Scripture is known through the church's decision, which when conciliar is infallible (as when the Council of Trent defined the Old Testament apocrypha into the canon, something never before done). Protestants said: The authority of church use and definition, though weighty, is not final nor divine; recognition of canonical Scripture depends ultimately on the covenanted inner witness of the Spirit, whereby the divine source and authority of those books which the church has historically attested to (not, therefore, the apocrypha) is made evident to faith.

On the second issue, Rome said: Scripture is not self-explanatory, and the Bible reader who does not let the teaching church tell him what the book means will err to his soul's hurt. Protestants said: Though it is true that God has appointed the preaching of the word as the prime means of Christian understanding, yet all things necessary to salvation are plain in the biblical text, so that the one who reads attentively, seeking the Spirit's help and comparing Scripture with Scripture, will not be led astray.

On the third issue Rome said: Scripture needs to be supplemented by traditions which the church hands down. Protestants replied: The absence of traditional items (papacy, penances, pilgrimages, what have you) from the Bible argues their non-necessity and probable unsoundness. Urged the Reformers: The basic form of the church's discipleship to its Lord is to echo Scripture in its confession and obey Scripture in its life, changing its present behavior in whatever way Scripture proves to require. Replied Rome: The church serves its Lord most truly by transmitting the whole deposit of faith and moral teaching found within its tradition, of which Scripture is only part. The debate has continued.

Within Protestantism things were complicated by the progressive outworking of two Renaissance motifs: man's intellectual autonomy, and his status as the measure of all things. These soon dissolved the frame of reference within which the Reformation debate took place. Both Rome and the Reformers were clear that this world depends on a Creator who rules and speaks, who governs its whole course and makes miraculous redemptive intrusions into it, and that both church and Bible are products of such intrusion—the former through regeneration, the latter by inspiration. But seventeenth-century deism, eighteenth-century rationalism, and nineteenth-century liberalism smudged this clarity within Protestantism, at least among its academics. Shut out of the world by deists, silenced by Kant's critical philosophy, and identified by Schleiermacher with what Lutheran pietists felt about him (a major scaling down), God so shrank in human minds that the miraculous realities of regeneration and inspiration became incredible. The church came to be seen as either a voluntary ethical association maintained by priestcraft in some cases and by state patronage in others, or as the state itself striking moral attitudes. The Bible was viewed as a testament of religion, a documentary record of how God was sought and found, containing more of men's spotty and uneven thoughts about God than of God's true and abiding thoughts about mankind. The function of Scripture, thus conceived, was to give the church moral inspiration and emotional encouragement, rather than to rule the church for God by mediating God's instruction and direction. In this way the Bible, which the Reformers venerated as in Calvin's phrase "the sceptre of God" (in other words the instrument of divine government), came to be regarded as an instrument of human culture. Among Protestant leaders the original Protestant understanding of biblical authority was almost wholly eclipsed.

In this century, the Bible-church relationship has become a major theme of discussion once more. As the turn-of-the-century optimism of religious and political liberals shrivelled in Europe and Britain through the impact of the First World War, and in North America a decade later through the impact of the Great Depression, Protestants began to realize afresh that the church is God's sinful, needy people living only by his word of grace, and that Scripture, which witnesses to God's word and work for his people in the past, is the trysting place where he meets and addresses his church today. The names of Barth, Brunner, and Reinhold Niebuhr call for honorable mention among exponents of this emphasis. Faith in Scripture as the record and medium of revelation revived, and faith in the living God of Scripture seemed to revive with it. In the 1940s "biblical theology" appeared, announcing itself as the discipline whereby one reads canonical Scripture "from within," as a corporate confession of faith in the God of redemptive history; one identifies with that faith; and one then tackles all questions of truth and obedience in directly biblical terms. Roman Catholic and ecumenical theologians took up "biblical theology," and many fine expositions of the Bible "from within" have been produced during the past fifty years. These works imparted to the church everywhere a more vivid sense of its continuity and identity with the church of the Old and New Testaments than Christian believers had known for many a long day.

Among scholars, however, "biblical theology" has for quite some time been under a cloud. Its assumption of the unity of biblical teaching is on the shelf while the hypothesis of an ultimate plurality of biblical theologies is explored. The instability and incoherence which marked this newborn discipline from the start, but which its first practitioners had hoped to transcend, are frequently and mercilessly highlighted. Its defects unfortunately are real, and go deep. As I pointed out in 1958,[1] the "biblical theology" program as presented by its architects suffers from unending oscillations because it refuses *a priori* to identify with the uniform biblical belief in totally trustworthy Scriptures, but rests on the standard type of academic biblical criticism which treats as possibly or actually false much that the Bible presents as true. This inconsistent streak of skepticism, violating the movement's own announced method, has, as I predicted,[2] become its Achilles' heel. From its own ranks have come scholars urging that theology must face the overall historical uncertainty of Scripture; that the overlay of interpretation in biblical narrative means we regularly cannot be sure what actually happened, i.e., what we could have seen and verified had we been there; that no one "biblical way of thinking" and no unique "Hebrew mentality" (as was once rashly claimed) can be shown to exist; that since different theologies and historical approaches, brought to Scripture, yield different interpretations of key points, biblical authority is hopelessly problematical; and that there is no good reason anyway to treat the fruits of historical exegesis and criticism as theologically normative.[3]

These problems of relating biblical narrative to historical fact and part to part within the Bible cannot be opened up here, but it can be said at once that they look insoluble on any other basis than that the canonical Scriptures are what the biblical writers and precritical expositors took them to be, namely God's witness to himself in the form of celebratory, reflective, and didactic witness by those who, "moved by the Holy Spirit spoke from God" (2 Pet. 1:21, RSV). On this basis, however, "biblical theology" can, I think, be put back on the road academically,[4] and this is certainly desirable, for when consistently pursued it is wholly right-minded. Plainly as an academic discipline it fell on its face through trying to go too far too fast and too unsteadily, without enough methodological reflection on what it was doing. Equally plainly, however, "biblical theology" is in essence the approach taken by the great body of theologically significant biblical expositors from Irenaeus in the second century to

Calvin in the sixteenth and Barth in the twentieth. Likewise, it is the technical statement of the approach which I have already outlined as the wayfarer's path to understanding.[5] So it needs to be rehabilitated, not abandoned.

In the meantime, the new biblical interest has borne many encouraging fruits. The Council of Trent was long thought to teach that unwritten traditions and the written Scriptures were two separate sources of divine truth, but now it has been shown that this is not necessarily so,[6] and Vatican II spoke of tradition as simply the church's deepening understanding of the Scriptures.[7] More and more Roman Catholic theologians, with Karl Rahner till his death the dean of them,[8] are recognizing an obligation to show that each particular tradition has an adequate biblical base. Major ecumenical studies of tradition have been made,[9] with Protestants showing a new interest in tradition as the initial exposition of Scripture which the church hands on to nurture each new generation. The stress which all denominations exhibit on lay Bible study and biblical preaching in worship testifies to a widespread sense that Scripture must, and can, renew the church—a sense, be it said, no less strong among Roman Catholics than among Protestants.[10] All these developments raise again the old problem: How should the proper relationship between Bible and church be formulated in theory, and how can it be realized in practice?

It will help us in discussing these questions if we first spend a little time defining our terms.

The Bible

What is *the Bible?* On the face of it, it is a library—a collection of sixty-six separate items, written in three languages (Hebrew, Aramaic, Greek), composed and brought together over a period of more than a thousand years, and containing material of the most varied literary types—written history, personal memoirs, sermons, letters, hymns, prayers, love poetry, philosophical poetry, family trees, visions, tales, statistics, public laws, rubrics for rituals, inventories, and much else. It divides into two collections, the second dating from a single half-century (hardly more, and perhaps much less) several hundred years after the composing of the first collection ended.

You might have expected this mass of material to be classified as a compendium of Jewish and Christian classics, or something like that. But nothing of the kind! From the start the Christian church has treated the two collections with their varied contents as a unified whole. It was doing this at the end of the first century, before it had a single name for them, when what we call the Old Testament was "the Scriptures" and what we call the New Testament was "the Gospel and the Apostles." For all the books to appear, as now they do, in a one thousand-plus-page volume called "the Holy Bible" (singular) makes explicit the view of their unity that was always implicit in the church's use of them.

The Christian idea of Scripture as the God-given *canon* (measuring rod, standard, ruler, rule) came from Judaism and the Old Testament. The church, taught by the apostles, claimed the Jewish Scriptures as written by divine inspiration to instruct Christians (cf. Rom. 15:4, cf. 3:2, 16:26; 1 Cor. 9:9 cf., 10:11; 1 Pet. 1:10-12); bracketed with them a selection of documents containing apostolic witness to

Christ (cf. 2 Pet. 3:16); and formed at once the habit of elucidating texts and establishing tenets by cross-reference to other parts of the whole collection, just as the rabbis, Jesus, and several New Testament authors had done in handling the Old Testament. This habit proclaims the assumption that the entire collection forms a unity.

Many, however, who have tried to read the Bible have got lost in it and found no way to put it all together; can the assumption of unity then be justified? The answer is yes, and at two distinct levels.

First, the sixty-six books have a demonstrable unity of subject matter and standpoint. This unity that links Genesis, Judges, Job, and Jeremiah with Matthew, Acts, Romans, and Revelation and all that lies between. Each book proves on inspection to be recounting or anticipating or reflecting on or giving thanks for part or all of the work of the Creator who is also the Redeemer and who acts to set up his kingdom of grace in and over human lives. This work of God in both the space-time continuum of world history and in his personal dealings with individuals is the story line of the Bible. The story has one hero (the triune Jehovah, Father, Son, and Holy Spirit), one theme (life for sinful mankind through Jesus Christ by faith), and a unified plot. Opening with tragedy (humankind pitchforked into ruin: the fall and the flood), the plot moves to a long episodic buildup (the call of Abraham and the career of his descendants; two captivities, one in Egypt and one in Babylon; two exoduses; an earthly kingdom that rises and wanes; and hope of an eternal kingdom that grows steadily stronger as human prospects wither). The climax comes with a catastrophic reversal of apparent disaster (the Son of God arrives and is killed; but he rises to reign, sends the Spirit, and pledges his return; through his atoning death sinners are saved, the kingdom of grace is fully revealed, and the woman's seed triumphs). The story locates our lives between Christ's two comings and directs us to trust him as our Savior, Lord, and Deliverer from the wrath to come (cf. 1 Thess. 1:10); it is thus *kerygma* (proclamation), the sum and substance of the gospel message. The story is also the reference point for books mainly of doctrine (e.g., Romans), mainly of ethics (e.g., Proverbs; Hosea; James), and mainly of devotion (e.g., the Psalms); you cannot understand these books properly till you slot them into their place in the history, on which in fact they are all in one way or another responsive comments, interpretative, celebratory, and applicatory. Read the Bible with something other than the ongoing story as your key, and you may well feel lost and wonder how it all hangs together. But read it in terms of the story, and amazement at its inner unity is likely to overwhelm you.

It was Irenaeus, reacting against Marcion and other Gnostics when they denied that the God of the Old Testament is identical with the God of the New, who in the second century pioneered the highlighting of the Bible's unity of plot. In our day "biblical theology," reacting against denials of redemptive continuity between the two Testaments, has highlighted the point again. As a result, presentations of the Bible as *narrative* (how God has worked), as *drama* (how our redemption was won), and as *witness* to the God who loves, seeks, and saves, has effectively displaced the older liberal account of it as a treasury of religious experience, the viewpoint embodied in such books as E. F. Scott's *Varieties of New Testament Religion* (1943). Whereas the first half of this century saw such publications as *The Bible Designed to Be Read as Literature* (a title which G. B. Bentley described as a gravestone for the word of God[11]), popular accounts of the Bible for the post-Second World War generation had titles like *The Book of the Acts of God* (G. Ernest Wright and Reginald Fuller).[12] The change reflected a great recovery of understanding.

Nor is this all. *In elucidating the unity of the Bible there is, second, the fact of inspiration to be reckoned with.* Scripture is God's own teaching!—that was Paul's meaning when he wrote in 2 Timothy 3:16 that all Scripture (he meant, our Old Testament) is *theopneustos* (God-breathed, a product of the creative breath which according to Psalm 33:6 made the heavens, in other words a work of the Holy Spirit, just as the specific Old Testament quotations in Mark 12:36; Acts 4:25-26, 28:25-27; Heb. 3:7-11, 10:15-17 are said to be).[13] To this conviction New Testament writers testify every time they cite an Old Testament passage as bringing Christians God's message.[14] Hereby they show their certainty that God gave these Scriptures by a special exercise of his providence in order to instruct "for salvation through faith in Christ Jesus," and equip for every good work, generations unborn at the time of writing (cf. 2 Tim. 3:15-17). That the books are fully human is not nor ever was in question; the point is that they are profitable for Christians because they have ultimately a divine origin and carry a divine message for Christians, having been given by God with Christians in mind. So what Peter says of the prophets—"men they were, but, impelled by the Holy Spirit, they spoke the words of God," 2 Pet. 1:21 (NEB: "what came from God" would be closer to the Greek than "the words of God," though the thought as paraphrased is right)—should be said of all Old Testament writers, whatever the literary type of their work and however it was composed.

It is clear that the psychological dimensions and phenomena of the process of divine inspiration varied from one writer to another, and from time to time for the same writer. Thus, the inspiration of the prophets delivering (and also recording or dictating, cf. Jer. 36) God's oracles was psychologically *dualistic*, in the sense that they knew themselves to be simply relaying what they had received, with no admixture of their own thoughts (whatever they might have contributed to the material's poetic form). The inspiration of the historians was psychologically *didactic*, in the sense that they evidently wrote on the basis of research into facts and traditions and reflection on the most instructive shape to give their material. Something similar should be said about the wisdom writers, and about the anonymous editors and redactors who worked to give the prophetic and historical books their final form. The inspiration of the psalmists and poets was psychologically *responsive* and *creative*, in the sense that they crafted into shape the praises and prayers and celebratory declarations that welled up within them as they looked towards God, just as do secular poets and song writers in working up their ideas for secular lyrics.

Here, then, were three quite different states of mind. The prophet would say, "God speaks through me, as his sounding board"; the historian and wisdom teacher would say, "I speak for God, as one who knows what he is talking about"; the psalmist and poet would say, "I speak in God's presence, as one who has felt the force of his truth and his touch." But the point to note is that whatever the psychological mode of inspiration, the theological reality of it was the same throughout. The books, like their authors, are fully human, but their message is also, and equally, divine.

New Testament inspiration is of the same three types: dualistic (Revelation), didactic (the Gospels, Acts and Epistles) and lyric (hymns and doxologies); each type corresponding closely to its Old Testament counterpart.

The inspiration of Scripture, as defined, is commonly regarded today as dubious and problematical, not to say incredible, but for New Testament Christians, teachers and taught alike, it was axiomatic. Why this difference? It is not enough to say that we are aware of critical questions about the truth of the Old Testament of which New Testament Christians were not aware; had they known of them, it would not have affected their attitude. For they had a compelling positive reason for accepting Scripture as instruction direct from their God. Not only was this view of Scripture basic to the Jewish faith out of which Christianity came, it was basic also to the ministry of Jesus himself. Jesus said, "Do not think that I have come to abolish the Law or the Prophets; I have not come to abolish them but to fulfill them" (Matt. 5:17). With this claim, which is in truth the hinge on which the whole New Testament view of Christianity turns, Jesus explicitly took his stand under the authority of Scripture; while differing from others on its interpretation at certain key points, he endorsed completely the received view of its nature and normative force, as *torah* (authoritative instruction) from the Creator, his

Father. The apostles did not fail to follow their Master here. As I wrote elsewhere:

> Christ and his apostles quote Old Testament texts not merely as what, e.g., Moses, David or Isaiah said (see Mk. 7:10, 12:36, 7:6; Rom. 10:5, 11:9, 10:20, etc.), but also as what God said through these men (see Acts 4:25, 28:25, etc.), or sometimes simply what "he" (God) says (e.g., 2 Cor. 6:16; Heb. 8:5, 8), or what the Holy Ghost says (Heb. 3:7, 10:15). Furthermore, Old Testament statements, not made by God in their contexts, are quoted as utterances of God (Mt. 19:4 f.; Heb. 3:7; Acts 13:34 f.; citing Gen. 2:24; Ps. 95:7; Is. 55:2 respectively). Also, Paul refers to God's promise to Abraham and his threat to Pharaoh, both spoken long before the biblical record of them was written, as words which *Scripture* spoke to these two men (Gal. 3:8; Rom. 9:17); which shows how completely he equated the statements of Scripture with the utterance of God.[15]

Clearly, it was as much part of New Testament Christianity to receive as divine teaching the Old Testament, which witnessed to Christ and which he fulfilled, as it was to receive as divine teaching the message of Jesus and his apostles.

It is indeed scarcely possible to account for the staggering unity of standpoint and subject matter on which I commented above without positing inspiration. Four centuries ago John Calvin appealed to the "beautiful harmony of all its parts"[16] as confirming belief in the Bible's divine origin and authority, and in this as in so much else Calvin's judgment was sound. There is no doubt that Calvin, who always treated biblical teaching as God's instruction and affirmed that all believers knew it to be so through the inner witness of the Spirit, held the view of inspiration outlined above.[17] It is ironic that in our time Reformed churches generally should have been so overawed by the supposedly sure results of biblical criticism (which, being loaded from the start with skeptical assumptions, could not but come up with skeptical conclusions) as largely to give up Calvin's view; doubly ironic when one observes that the most recent ecclesiastical witness to it of any standing has been borne by the Church of Rome! The statement of Vatican II on biblical inspiration merits quotation in full.

11. Those divinely revealed realities which are contained and presented in sacred Scripture have been committed to writing under the inspiration of the Holy Spirit. Holy Mother Church, relying on the belief of the apostles, holds that the books of both the Old and New Testaments in their entirety, with all their parts, are sacred and canonical because, having been written under the inspiration of the Holy Spirit (cf. Jn. 20:31; 2 Tim. 3:16; 2 Pet. 1:19-21; 3:15-16) they have God for their author and have been handed on as such to the Church herself. In composing the sacred books, God chose men, and while employed by him they made use of their own powers and abilities; thus with him acting in them and through them, they, as true authors, consigned to writing everything and only those things which he wanted.

Therefore, since everything asserted by the inspired authors or sacred writers must be held to be asserted by the Holy Spirit, it follows that the books of Scripture must be acknowledged as teaching firmly, faithfully, and without error that truth which God wanted put into the sacred writings for the sake of our salvation. Therefore "all Scripture is inspired by God and useful for teaching, for reproving, for correcting, for instruction in righteousness; that the man of God may be perfect, equipped for every good work" (2 Tim. 3:16-17). . . .

13. In sacred Scripture, therefore, while the truth and holiness of God always remain intact, the marvelous "condescension" of eternal wisdom is clearly shown, "that we may learn the gentle kindness of God, which words cannot express, and how far he has gone in adapting his language with thoughtful concern for our weak human nature." For the words of God, expressed in human language, have been made like human discourse, just as of old the Word of the eternal Father, when he took to himself the weak flesh of humanity, became like other men.[18]

Sadly, some Roman Catholic theologians twist the second of these paragraphs to mean "limited inerrancy"—that is, that not everything in Scripture is "truth which God wanted put into the sacred writings for the sake of our salvation," and that what does not come in that category cannot always be trusted.[19] Yet in itself, naturally understood, this is as fine a statement of what Protestants and Roman Catholics once held in common as one could wish for. It will be a happy day when Protestants again confess the truth about Scripture in terms like these, grounding its unity of subject matter in the unity of God, its primary author.

Such is the Bible. What, now, do we mean when we speak of the church?

Church

In the New Testament the church is a many-sided reality which is spoken of from various points of view. In this chapter, however, the viewpoint is precise and constant. By the church I mean, not "the whole number of the elect" (to quote the Westminster Confession, xxv.i), nor the organized regional or denominational federations (the Church of South India, the Anglican church, the Assemblies of God or whatever), but the pilgrim people of God on earth as such. The church is that historically continuous society which traces its lineage back to the apostles and the day of Pentecost, and behind that to Abraham, father of the faithful, whose "seed" the church is through faith in and union with Abraham's primary seed, Jesus Christ (cf. Rom. 4:16; Gal. 3:7-20). It is God's adopted family of children and heirs, bound to him as he is bound to it in the bonds of his gracious covenant. It is also the body and bride of Jesus Christ, the "company of faithful men" (coetus fidelium: the phrase comes from Anglican Article 19) who enjoy union and communion with the Mediator through the Holy Spirit. As Luther rightly said, the church is essentially invisible, an object of faith rather than of sight, for the realities which constitute it—the glorified Christ who is its head, and faith which embraces him, and the Spirit who unites us with him and communicates his gifts to us—are not open to observation nor detectable by any physical test at present, whatever may become the case when Christ returns. But the church becomes visible in its local assemblies, each of which is the body of Christ in manifestation, an outcrop, specimen, sample, and microcosm of the church as a whole. It becomes visible by its association, fellowship, discipline, and witness, by the preaching and sharing of God's Word which it sponsors, by its administering of the sacraments of entry and continuance according to Christ's command, and by its commitment to the work which the Master gave it to do.

Now it is the nature of the church to live under the authority of Jesus Christ as its teacher no less than as its king and its priest. The church depends on the Lord Jesus for instruction in spiritual things, and looks to the Spirit of Jesus to teach it these things in the Savior's name. This is true of both "Catholic" and "Protestant" outlooks. The standard Roman Catholic claim is that the church (defined, of course, in terms of communion with the Pope), being the extension of the incarnation, the prolonging in space and time of Christ's presence in this world, actually partakes of the divine infallibility and teaching authority that belong to the Lord himself. These qualities, according to the theory, find definitive expression when the Pope speaking *ex cathedra* (that is, in his official character as the teacher of Christendom exercising his *magisterium,* or teaching office) confirms the declarations of councils or in his own person defines convictions which the Holy Spirit is held to have established in the church's corporate mind. Eastern Orthodoxy and Anglo-Catholicism, while rejecting the doctrine of the papacy, appeal similarly to the authority of the church's corporate mind down the ages ("holy Tradition").

It is important to see that these appeals to the church for

doctrine, which to Protestants might look like ways of manufacturing truths and facts (lineal apostolic succession, localized eucharistic presence, the papal office itself, the Immaculate Conception and Assumption of Mary, etc.) contrary to the Spirit's teaching from Scripture, are actually expressions, however mistaken, of the same concern to be taught by Jesus Christ which makes Protestants pore over the Bible. That "man shall not live by bread alone, but by every word that proceeds from the mouth of God" (Matt. 4:4, citing Deut. 8:3, RSV) is common ground; the difference is over how God teaches.

There can be no disputing that churchmanship means discipleship, and discipleship means learning, and learning means listening to the word of the Lord. Luther defined the church in a way that, he claimed, a child of seven could grasp! He defined it as "those who hear the shepherd's voice" (an echo, of course, of John 10:27). Concern to hear Christ's voice and be taught by him is basic to the identity of both the Christian and the church.

The Bible is the book of the church; the church is the people of the book. What, now, is the proper relation between the Bible and the church?

In answer, I offer these two propositions: first, *it is for the Bible to form and reform the church*; second, *it is for the church to keep and keep to the Bible*. Let us explore them in order in what follows.

The Bible Over the Church

It is for the Bible to form and reform the church. This assertion breaks down into four.

First, the church's corporate life must be shaped by the gospel. By "gospel" (literally, "the news," "the good news") I mean here the whole "word of God" which the apostles preached and taught, embodying the "word of God" which came from Jesus (cf. Luke 5:1, 8:11, 21, 11:28; Acts 4:31, 8:14, 11:1, 13:7, 44, 46; Col. 1:25; 1 Thess. 2:13; 1 Tim. 2:9). In other words, the gospel is the whole Christian message: the facts of Jesus' life, death, rising, reign, and future return, his missionary commission, institution of the sacraments, and sending of the Spirit (for which see the Gospels and Acts), plus Old Testament facts forming the background (as recounted in, e.g., Gal. 3–4; Rom. 4, 9–11; Hebrews), plus theological analysis, with ethical corollaries, of God's eternal plan of grace, his "whole counsel" which has Christ and the church at its heart (Acts 20:27, RSV; see the church Epistles).

By responding to the Bible's message with faith, that is, credence and commitment, the church comes to exist in God's presence as a company of believers and to take form locally as a visibly organized fellowship. Anglican Article 19 defines the visible church as "a congregation of faithful men, in the which the pure Word of God is preached, and the Sacraments be duly ministered according to Christ's ordinance in all those things that of necessity are requisite to the same." It is thus specifying that the New Testament message must shape the faith, life, and order of God's pilgrim people at all points.

Protestants have differed as to how far New Testament descriptions of early church life have prescriptive force for church life now in such matters as liturgy, ministerial order, and synods. What is at issue here, however, is interpreta-

tion, not authority. On the decisiveness of biblical principles there has been agreement. The debate has had to do
only with what those principles are—whether the New
Testament should be read as setting forth by precept and
precedent a universally required church order, as some
Presbyterians, Baptists, and Christian Brethren have
thought; or as leaving the church freedom (and so imposing on it responsibility) to implement general principles
about church fellowship and ministry in the way that
seems best in our situation, which is how other Presbyterians, with Anglicans and Lutherans and Methodists, have
seen the matter and how the New Testament Christians
seemed to see it. But all Protestants agree that neither their
own church order nor any other can be justified save as a
direct response to New Testament teaching. Responsive
conformity to Christ and his gospel is acknowledged by
all, as was said above, to be the very foundation and essence of the church's identity.

Second, our only access to the gospel is through the Scriptures.
This is first a historical point: the New Testament books are
the prime witnesses to what Christ and the apostles taught.
They are authentic and responsible sources, contemporary
or near-contemporary with the events recorded,[20] and no
other independent sources of any significance are available.[21] But it is also a theological point: the New Testament,
as we saw, is Spirit-inspired apostolic witness, and Christ
meant this witness to fix the church's faith for all time. That
is implied, as we saw earlier, by his prayer, "I do not pray
for these only, but also for those who believe in me *through
their word*" (John 17:20, RSV).

Historically, as Protestant apologists urge against Rome,

no one can tell if post-apostolic traditions, allegedly apostolic in origin, really are so. Theologically, says Oscar Cullmann, the mid-second-century recognition of apostolic writings as *canonical*—that is, as the decisive rule for faith and life—shows clear awareness that post-apostolic tradition and apostolic tradition are not on a par, but that the latter must control and correct the former. Here are Cullmann's words:

> By establishing the *principle* of a Canon the Church . . . drew a line under the apostolic tradition. She declared implicitly that from that very moment every subsequent tradition must be submitted to the control of the apostolic tradition. In other terms, she declared: here is the tradition which *constituted* the Church, which imposed itself on her. . . . To establish a Canon is equivalent to recognizing: henceforth our ecclesiastical tradition needs to be controlled; with the help of the Holy Spirit it will be controlled by the apostolic tradition fixed in writing. . . . To fix a canon was to say: henceforth we renounce the right to consider as a norm other traditions that are not fixed by the Apostles in writing. . . . To say that the writings brought together in a Canon should be considered as *norm* was to say that they should be considered as *sufficient*. The teaching office of the Church was not abdicated by this final act of fixing the Canon, but its future activity was made to depend on a norm that was superior.[22]

To feel the full force of Cullmann's point, we should note that the early church's concern in thus affirming the authority of apostolic tradition stemmed from its concerns for the gospel and salvation rather than for church organization and law. In other words: the concern was not just for an official orthodoxy, but for the personal knowledge of salvation in Christ to which "sound words" (1 Tim. 6:3, RSV; 2 Tim. 1:13; cf. Rom. 6:17) lead. By setting apostolic writings above all other tradition, the early church was consciously guarding the gospel against its perverters. In ascribing to those writings divine authority, it was both bracketing them with the Old Testament as "able to instruct you for salvation through faith in Christ Jesus" (2 Tim. 3:15, RSV) and aligning itself with the New Testament congregations whose obedience to the apostolic message had actually brought them salvation.

To see the canonizing process, as some seem to do, as the post-apostolic church meeting its own felt need of a court of appeal, and to consider on that basis how providence, the Spirit, study, and church authority combined to give us the books we now have, is to miss the essence of what went on. Essentially, what was happening was this: the apostolic message about redemption, which was and is part of the saving fact of Christ, was authenticating itself as from God in its written form, just as it had authenticated itself when first preached in Jerusalem, Samaria, Corinth, and Rome. Christ had authorized the apostles to declare this message with his authority, and so by the Spirit they did, both orally and in writing. The church's historic recognition of written apostolic witness as the New Testament canon means essentially that the church acknowledges it to be God's word of salvation. Inquiry into the pedigree, use, and contents of particular books can make it seem reasonable to accept them as authentic and unreasonable not to, but ultimately the church's acceptance of them in each generation is because they impose themselves—because, that is, the church hears in them the saving word of God.

Ridderbos focuses this by distinguishing between the canon viewed qualitatively (as the authentic, authoritative presentation of Christ) and quantitatively (as a fixed collection of books).[23] The "quantitative" question, which books should be in the collection, has prompted debate, on and off, since the second century; but the "qualitative" question, whether written apostolic witness to Christ and salvation should be a norm for all Christians, was never disputed till modern times (when all first principles, it seems, are disputed by someone or other!). No felt uncertainties or scholars' disputes about the extent of the canon, therefore, should be thought to invalidate the principle that the church's knowledge of the gospel comes ultimately through the Scriptures alone.[24]

In saying this, I do not suggest for one moment that traditions of teaching, worship, and order in the church are unimportant. On the contrary, they should be gratefully received and respectfully handled, for they are the fruit of much past effort to think and live biblically, and much of their content is plainly the result of the Spirit's teaching and application of Scripture (the ecumenical creeds, for instance, and a great deal of the local confessions, liturgies, hymns, and theological and devotional writing that particular parts of the church have produced). To say that "tradition represents the worldliness of the Church"[25] is one-sided; tradition is not always worldly and wrong. Yet the statement has a point: tradition is not always godly and right either. This is what you would expect where the Spirit is really at work among sinners who are not yet perfectly sanctified in either head or heart.

This is why all traditions must be submitted to the corrective judgment of the Scriptures which they seek to expound and apply and subserve: why, in particular, post-apostolic traditions must be brought under the control of apostolic tradition in the New Testament. As Paul in Christ's name challenged the Jerusalem church tradition which called for the circumcision of Gentile converts in Galatia and the "human tradition" which was corrupting the doctrine, worship, and service of God through Christ at Colossae (Col. 2:8); as also our Lord in his Father's name challenged the rabbinic expository tradition as corrupting and evading the divine law (cf. Mark 7:5-13; Matt. 5:20-48); so Paul and his fellow witnesses who wrote the New Testament, and Christ himself speaking in and through them, must be allowed to challenge our own latter-day traditions. Only that which is demonstrably rooted in Scripture, and which therefore we can be sure the apostles would have endorsed, can be held to belong to the gospel, or to be needed for personal spiritual health or the church's corporate pleasing of God.

Third, the Scriptures interpret themselves clearly to the people of God through the Holy Spirit. It is sad to find a Protestant author declaring that "as the Roman Church has clearly and consistently taught, the Bible needs an interpreter; it does not bear its plain meaning on its face."[26] The statement is not even half true. The testimony both of Protestant history over four and a half centuries and also of the ecumenical biblical movement till very recently[27] is that those who will read the Bible "from within," letting it speak for itself in its own terms, reach remarkable unanimity as to its meaning.[28] Nor should this surprise us, for the inspired books were written not to mystify but to be understood, and the Spirit who gave them is with the church to interpret them, by enabling us to grasp their message in its application to ourselves. The Reformers spoke in this connection of the *clarity* or *perspicuity* of Scripture. They were not denying that Scripture sometimes alludes to things of which we have insufficient knowledge fully to explain the reference (e.g., baptism for the dead at Corinth, 1 Cor. 15:29; the "man of sin" in 2 Thess. 2:3, etc.); nor were they denying that secondary and incidental matters in Scripture are sometimes less than clear. Their point was that the main things, the things that the writers themselves were concerned to stress, are so fully and plainly presented that none who bring to the Bible an honest willingness to meet and know God, and to be changed by him, will miss them. The discovery that on the essentials Scripture can speak for itself was one mainspring of the Reformation, and has animated evangelical religion ever since. To allege at this stage of history that the Bible "does not bear its plain meaning on its face" is rather like complaining that television sets do not work. Millions can testify that they work very well if you know how to switch them on.

Fourth, the church, once formed, needs constantly to be reformed by the Bible. We have already reminded ourselves that the believers who make the church are a community of imperfectly sanctified sinners; now we should link with that the New Testament vision of the church as under constant attack from "principalities ... powers ... world rulers of this present darkness . . . spiritual hosts of wickedness in the heavenly places" (Eph. 6:12, RSV), and we should face the certainty that the church in this and every age will have cause to acknowledge that it has slipped and failed. Lapses into the deformity of misbelief and unbelief, ethical error and compromise, apathy and superstition, formality and dead routine, must be expected. So reformation, not only in the negative sense of purging abuses (for man cannot live on disinfectant alone) but also in the positive sense of re-forming, or re-shaping, through the giving of new scriptural substance to faith and life, will be our chronic need. The old slogan *ecclesia reformata semper reformanda* (the reformed church always needs to be reformed) bears true witness to this.

The deforming of the church is a constant problem, and a much bigger one than is sometimes recognized. It is not just a matter of doctrine, though where (for instance) the divinity of Jesus or the objectivity of his atoning sacrifice or his bodily resurrection or Paul's doctrine of justification by faith or John's idea of regeneration are denied, the revised version of Christianity that results will be a grievous distortion. Nor is it just a matter of ethics, though where (for instance) husbands are encouraged to treat their wives as horses to be broken in or doormats to be trodden on, or homosexual partnerships are treated as the equivalent of Christian marriage, lives will end up very much damaged and out of shape, within the church no less than outside it. But a congregation may be entirely orthodox in faith and correct in its moral code and still lack missionary and evangelistic passion, and ardor in worship, and a corporate concern for holiness, and a social conscience, and a caring heart, and a loving focus on the glory of the Father, the Son, and the Holy Spirit. These are as truly disfigurements and disorders as outright heresy and immorality would be. Sin and Satan keep combining to deform the life of the church, and reformation—the re-shaping of what is out of shape, and the re-invigorating of what has gone dead—is a continual need.

Today's words for what I have called reformation are *renewal* and *revival,* and "reformation" is widely thought of as a less vital process, having to do with externals only; but "reformation" on sixteenth- and seventeenth-century lips meant all that these terms mean and more, and I shall stay with the word in making my present point.

Can Scripture in these days reform and revitalize moribund churches—which means first and foremost, the moribund individuals who make them up? It may be a sufficient answer to point out that by the Spirit's power Scripture has certainly done this in the past. Think, for instance, of some of the movements sparked off by the Spirit's application—first to individuals, then through them to communities—of just one book, filling between fifteen and twenty pages in most Bibles, Paul's letter to the Romans. Calvin described it as "a sure road . . . to the understanding of the whole Scripture," and surely he was right.

Augustine, troubled but uncommitted, read in a friend's Bible Romans 13:14: "Put on the Lord Jesus Christ, and make no provision for the flesh" (RSV). He tells us that then "a clear light flooded my heart, and all the darkness of doubt vanished away."[29] A thoroughgoing Christian from that moment on, he became the foremost champion of

God's free grace and the most influential teacher bar none in Western Christian history to date.

Then, eleven centuries later, there came Martin Luther, a monk and academic theologian, but a man without peace. He had found Romans baffling because he took "the righteousness of God" (Rom. 1:17, RSV) to be God's retributive righteousness judging sin (cf. Rom. 1:32; 2:5). Then he came to see that in Paul's usage in Romans this phrase really means "that righteousness whereby, through grace and sheer mercy, he justifies us by faith"—and at once, he reports, "I felt myself to be reborn and to have gone through open doors into paradise."[30] From this discovery came the teaching that triggered all the Reformation.

Two centuries after that, John Wesley, a failed missionary, heard Luther's Preface to Romans read at a meeting in London and tells us: "I felt my heart strangely warmed. I felt I did trust in Christ, Christ alone, for my salvation; and an assurance was given me that he had taken *my* sins away, even *mine*; and saved me from the law of sin and death."[31] From this experience of assurance sprang the momentous ministry that produced world Methodism.

Again in 1816 Robert Haldane expounded Romans to students in Geneva, and revival (reformation!) came to the Reformed churches of Switzerland and France; and in 1918 Karl Barth published an exposition of Romans that changed the course of twentieth-century theology. "There is no telling what may happen," wrote F. F. Bruce, "when people begin to study the Epistle to the Romans."[32] Nor is there any reason to think that the power of Romans, with the other Scriptures, to reform and revitalize Christians and churches, is any less today than it was—which means that a challenge confronts us here and now to seek in order that we may find. When you have finished reading this book, what is the next thing you will set yourself to do?

This leads to my second proposition. As it is for the Bible to form and reform the church, so *it is for the church to keep and keep to the Bible.* Consider the two points involved.

The Church Under the Bible

First, the church must keep the Bible. This is a Reformation point. As we saw, the Bible is our only sure link with apostolic Christianity, and the only sure means whereby God's word comes to us today. It is the handiwork, gift, and textbook of the Holy Spirit, and the instrument of our Lord's royal authority. Just as the Jews were entrusted with "the oracles of God" in Old Testament times (Rom. 3:2, RSV), so the Christian church is called to be, in the words of Anglican Article 20, "a keeper of Holy Writ." We have already noted that God, not the church, created the canon of Scripture. He inspired the books and moved the church to receive them for what they are. The church no more created the canon than Newton created the law of gravity; recognition is not creation. Barth's dictum states, "The Bible constitutes itself the Canon . . . because it imposed itself upon the church as such, and continually does so." This has been criticized as an oversimplification,[33] but it has the same sort of clarifying thrust as does the definition of engine-drivers (North Americans would say, engineers) as a class of individuals whose task it is to stop trains in scheduled places at scheduled times. The church must see itself, therefore, as neither author nor lord of Scripture, but as

steward of it, serving God both by observing in its own life
his written requirements and also by spreading Bible truth
as widely as possible so that all may learn "this message of
salvation" (Acts 13:26).

So Holy Writ is to be kept not under a bushel, but under
people's noses. Its message is to be held forth as diligently
as it is held fast. Churches must use all means to promote
individual and corporate attention to the Bible; to recover
the Bible-proclaiming, Bible-teaching ethos which was one
secret of all the strength they ever had; to foster group and
family Bible study; to sponsor good, clear translations and
expositions; and to bring the Bible to bear on theoretical
problems and practical decisions alike. The church serves
its Master best by keeping the Bible, not in store on the
shelf as a relic of the past, but in use in each congregation
as the ever-relevant handbook of authentic discipleship,
received in effect from the Master himself as his means of
fulfilling the divine promise and purpose of "teaching . . .
reproof . . . correction and . . . training in righteousness." So
any congregation in which Bibles are not in worshipers'
hands at services, nor used as the focus of attention in
sermons, nor studied as a main activity, has cause to be
ashamed of the poor quality of its discipleship.

Second, the church must keep to the Bible. "Do not merely
listen to the word, and so deceive yourselves," wrote
James. "Anyone who listens to the word but does not do
what it says is like a man who looks at his natural face in a
mirror . . . and . . . goes away and immediately forgets what
he looks like" (James 1:22-25). Only doers are blessed.
"Doing the word" then—"living by the truth," "obeying
his commands," "obeying his word" in John's phrases

(1 John 1:6, 2:3, 5)—is the church's calling. Nothing less—
no amount of idle and empty talk, however orthodox—will
please God or bring us good. There must be obedience.

Here, however, a painful problem emerges. To "do the
word" we must first understand it, and on biblical interpretation today the church is agonizingly divided. Hence
what some see as "doing the word" in fields of sexual,
medical, industrial, and political ethics is to others blatant
and destructive disobedience to the word, just as what
some today regard as biblical faith strikes others as antibib-
lical unbelief. The bewildering theological confusion, the
anarchic intellectual individualism, that plagues the modern church, both Protestant and Catholic, springs directly
from disagreement about the way to interpret Scripture—
that is, about the way to get at, not just its historical meaning, but what it means *for us*. Why this chaos of claims and
counterclaims? asks the bemused observer. What goes on?
In a nutshell, the answer is as follows.

As long as the belief in inspiration spelled out earlier in
this essay was the basis of interpretative endeavor, only
three divergences of principle and method were found
among biblical expositors.

1. Most church fathers and medievals thought that God's
message to each generation in and through the words of
Scripture was sometimes, if not always, cast into a code of
allegorical equivalents, which it was their task to crack; but
the Reformers and their followers have insisted that God's
message is always found in some application of the natural
meaning which the human writer's first readers would
have gleaned from his words. So, for instance, Protestant
interpreters urge that Jesus' Good Samaritan story is

simply a lesson about neighbor-love and reject the long-entrenched idea that it is the Catholic version of the gospel in disguise, the Jew being the sinner, the Samaritan being Jesus, the inn being the church, the two coins being the sacraments of Baptism and the Eucharist, and in some versions the innkeeper being the pope.

2. Roman Catholics held that we may read into Scripture from tradition meanings which the biblical words are capable of bearing in themselves (in relation, for instance, to the papacy or the Eucharist); but Protestants maintained that we must always confine ourselves to reading out of Scripture the meaning which the words demonstrably do bear in their context. So, for example, they decline to read "on this rock I will build my church" (Matt. 16:18) as Christ's sanctioning of papal primacy. They point out, first, that the "rock" may well be faith, and not Peter at all, and, second, that even if it is Peter, Jesus says nothing about Petrine succession.

3. Some Presbyterians, Puritans, and Christian (Plymouth) Brethren thought that all New Testament references to acceptable action taken in the apostolic churches have the force of command to later churches to do the same as part of their own church order; but other Protestants have not thought so. The former see Scripture as the "regulative" principle which, by not envisaging, for instance, the diocesan (i.e., area) bishop, in effect forbade him to exist; the latter see Scripture as the normative principle, giving the theology that all the church's managerial and ministerial arrangements must ever express.

All particular differences of understanding used to be located within the parameters which these three divergences set. But since biblical criticism got into its stride and Protestants started reading Scripture as relaying human thoughts rather than God's teaching, the possibilities of interpretative difference have greatly multiplied, and the task of discerning what each such difference implies has become far harder. In terms of approach and method there are nowadays, broadly speaking, three main types of interpreters.

1. There are those, Protestant and Catholic, who uphold the church's historic belief in biblical inspiration. Beyond that, they divide among themselves along the old lines. These conservatives mean by interpretation applying to ourselves the doctrinal and moral instruction of the Bible, read as an historically structured, self-authenticating and self-interpreting organism of revealed truth. Patristic expositor-theologians like Chrysostom and Augustine, and Protestant expositor-theologians like John Calvin, John Owen, Matthew Henry, Charles Hodge, William Hendriksen, and the great if strange Karl Barth, have gone this way. It is essentially the approach which Childs calls "canonical," and defends as such. (Childs, like Barth, declines to ground the instrumentality of Scripture in mediating God's word to his people on an inspiration which entails the inerrancy of Scripture as given; but Barth, at least, always treated Scripture as inerrant in every aspect of its witness to God's facts and their meanings, and he who does this cleaves in practice to the method we are describing here, even if his theoretical account of it falls short and his theology raises other problems.)

2. There are those, Protestant and Catholic, who view Scripture as witness to God by godly men who, though

they thought wrongly of him at some points, thought rightly and profoundly of him at others. The fallibility of the witnesses, which some highlight and others play down, is universally allowed for, and arguments are constantly being mounted from the coherence of this or that assertion with the mainstream of biblical thought to justify accepting the assertion as true. The (curious?) basis of the reasoning is that the Bible as a whole can't be wrong, though individual contributors to it can. However, tracing out the historical growth and coherence of biblical testimony is an important exercise in its own right, and it is all gain that expositors of this school work so hard at it, however little the skepticism that sets them going may seem justifiable.

These moderns mean by interpretation the distinguishing of true views of God and life from the rest of what is in the Bible—isolating its core, essence, overall thrust, or central witness, as they would say—and applying to us what they have selected. Their canon of truth and wisdom is thus narrower than the canon of Scripture, and their decisions as to which biblical assertions to discard and which biblical absolutes to relativize are bound to seem arbitrary both to colleagues who, operating on the same principle make different decisions, and to those who allow weight to the claim that (not some but) all Scripture is God-breathed. The approach I am describing is essentially that of the temporarily derailed "biblical theology" movement, of which Childs wrote: "One of the major factors in the breakdown . . . was its total failure to come to grips with the inspiration of Scripture. The strain of using orthodox Biblical language for the constructive part of theology, but at the same time approaching the Bible with all the assumptions of liberalism, proved in the end to cause an impossible tension."[34] Sadly, the large ecumenical community of scholars who still follow this method seem not to see the intrinsic oddity of what they are doing when they pick and choose within the Bible; it is of course always hard to discern oddity in an accepted communal activity.

3. There are those, mainly though not invariably Protestant, for whom the New Testament (the Old is a separate problem) is a culturally determined verbalization of ineffable existential encounters with God. These interpreters make two assumptions: The first is that God does not communicate with us through language; the second is that biblical thoughts about relations with him are "mythological" constructs in the sense that they function not as windows through which we watch God at work and so learn his ways, but as mirrors in which we see reflected the minds of the men whose encounters with God the myths objectify. What we learn from this is precisely their "self-understanding"—which, indeed, we may then come to share as our living though voiceless Creator similarly encounters us. This is the theme of Bultmannian hermeneutics, on which busy scholars have rung many changes in our time. The exponents of this "new hermeneutic," as it has been called, see interpretation as the task of so explicating the biblical verbal matrix by historical exegesis and so manipulating it in sermons as to promote in folk at the receiving end the same sort of subjective events that first produced it. They insist that one can only witness to encounter with God by mythology, which expresses and may spark off a new self-understanding, but which tells nothing about God save that he produced the self-understanding.

My line of argument in this book implies that the church can only in principle keep to the Bible as it interprets Scripture by method 1 (see p. 91). Methods 2 and 3 embody grains of truth which exponents of method 1 must never forget—that Scripture is no less human for being inspired, for instance, and that its verbal form is culturally conditioned everywhere—but as alternatives to method 1 they fail. Those who espouse them do so in good faith subjectively, but that does not alter the fact that they cannot yield good faith objectively. Where they dominate, truth and power fail, churchmen live in the dark spiritually, neither the triune God nor the gospel nor God's moral will are clearly known, and deadening and destructive confusion reigns, both in beliefs and in morals. We see this around us today. Both faithfulness and fruitfulness depend on adhering to method 1.

This is a sad conclusion, for much of the church today is effectively committed to these more or less mistaken methods, and a great part of the academic theological community lines up to stop people embracing method 1 as God-wrought spiritual instinct would lead them to do, lest they lapse into some form of obscurantism. To be sure, there has sometimes been obscurantism among simple adherents of method 1, just as there has been among sophisticated exponents of methods 2 and 3; but to blackball method 1 on this account is like forbidding us to go out and walk in the sunshine for fear that while doing so we might fall and break a leg, as someone we know once did. The truth is that if the church is ever again going to live happily and fruitfully with the Bible—which means, happily and fruitfully with its Lord, who rules by means of the

Bible—it must stop retreating from the ghost of an un-theological inerrancy, and once more embrace the whole Bible as the written word of God and interpret it on the basis that it neither misinforms nor misleads.

When Harold Lindsell put the finger on teaching institutions in the U.S. which had recently given up their corporate commitment to method 1,[35] he touched only the tip of the iceberg. Most centers where the church's future salaried instructors are trained gave up any such commitment long ago. Lindsell was right to focus on seminaries; what they are today the whole church is likely to be tomorrow. Seminaries and theological colleges are strategic places. The church will not learn to handle Scripture aright while budding clergy are taught to handle it wrongly.

Only by the grace of God through the Bible does the church ever learn to keep to the Bible. It is plain that the church needs much of that grace today. Whether Scripture will effectively re-establish its authority over the modern church remains to be seen. Vindicating the principle of "canonical" inerrancy, that is, an inerrancy shaped by exegesis and theology rather than by secular preoccupations, is a beginning, but no more.[36] The vagaries of current critical and hermeneutical opinion are desperately daunting, yet it is clear that desire to hear the Word of God from Scripture, and to know its enlivening power, burns strong in Christian hearts all around the world, and this is a hopeful sign. Perhaps the present pages may do something under God to deepen and direct that desire. Certainly, they could fulfill no higher ministry in the church at this time.

3

A LONG WAR
Fifty Years Battling for the Bible

This chapter tells a tale of events that I was privileged to observe at fairly close quarters, and in some of which I played a small part. At the risk of indulging an egotism that would be better mortified, I here narrate this story in some detail, partly to show my readers where I "come from," as we say, and partly because these events may have significance for the future. The Puritan Richard Baxter, who across a three-hundred-year gap has been a sort of mentor to me in a number of ways, diligently chronicled the events of his own time, proclaiming himself a hater of false history who wanted the true facts known. Same here! And if readers find my reminiscences trivial, they have my full permission to skip them. For what they are worth, however, I present them now.

For the best part of half a century, first in Britain and then in North America, I with many others have been expounding and defending the authority of the Bible as God's true Word, the trustworthy and sufficient rule of

faith. All that time I have known myself called to presby-
terial ministry, that is, to be a shepherd of God's flock, and I
have fought this good fight (for such I have taken it to be)
primarily for the furthering of pastoral goals: healthy spiritual life, strong churches, and vigorous outreach with the
gospel. I see biblical authority as methodologically the
most basic of theological issues. And I have fought for it,
not just for the sake of confessional orthodoxy or theological certainty or evangelical integrity or epistemological
sanity or to counter dehumanizing irrationalisms, though
all those concerns have entered into what I have done. But
my affirmation and defense of Holy Scripture has been first
and foremost for the sake of pastoral and evangelistic ministry, genuine godliness, the maturing of the church, and
spiritual revival. By these things the glory of God and the
good of human beings are most truly advanced, and they
simply are not found where the Bible does not have its
proper place in Christians' lives.

It is no news that not all who are called to academic
work have a pastoral motivation, just as not all who are
called to pastoral work have academic sensitivity to questions of truth.[1] But I, for one, feel the constraint of both
concerns together. So my goal in dogmatics is to find pure
streams and to strain out sewage; in communication, to
relay tested truth for believers to embrace and feed on as
their own; and in polemics, to keep such communication
from being obstructed by mental mistakes. One of my
readers once told me that all my writings were spirituality
really, and no estimate could be more congenial; but the
constant burden on my conscience as I write has always
been to find, focus, and further God's truth.

My story starts at Oxford University in 1944. Having been brought to faith in Jesus Christ out of empty religious formalism, I began devouring Scripture devotionally. When I had read it before, it had seemed uninteresting, but now it glowed and spoke. At the close of a Bible exposition forty-one days after my conversion, I found myself certain, quite suddenly, that the Bible was not, as I had previously thought, a mixture of history, legend and opinion, requiring selective treatment as other human miscellanies do. I knew now that it was in its own nature a divine production as well as a channel of divine communication, triggering insight and praise.

Years later, when I found Calvin saying that through the inward witness of the Holy Spirit every Christian experiences Scripture speaking authoritatively as from God,[2] I rejoiced to think that, without any prior human instruction and certainly without any prior acquaintance with Calvin, I had long known that experience. When, later still, I found Cornelius Van Til characterizing the Bible by saying that Christ, his Lord, had written him a letter,[3] my heart spoke its own "Amen" once more. The truth is that one element of the universal Christian experience into which the Bible leads is precisely the experience of the Bible challenging our thought and will with God's authority, and of our own inward inability to deny its divinity as it does so. That experience, by grace, has been mine throughout my Christian life—and is so still.

Evangelical Testimony

In the fifties I often addressed student and church groups

on biblical authority. When I was asked to write up a talk I had given rebutting a series of attacks by church leaders on what they called "our English fundamentalism" (specified by some as the religion of Inter-Varsity Fellowship reinforced by Billy Graham), what came out of the hopper was a full-length book that brought together much of what I had been saying over those years. Its title (apt enough, I think, though devised by the publisher, not me) was *"Fundamentalism" and the Word of God,*[4] a defiant echo of the title of Gabriel Hebert's critique, *Fundamentalism and the Church of God,* published the previous year.[5]

In his censuring of conservative evangelicals for obscurantist incompetence in biblical study and self-sufficient tunnel vision in religious relationships, Hebert had traversed well-worn territory. Throughout the twentieth century evangelicals on both sides of the Atlantic had been execrated as the awkward squad in God's church, for three reasons. First, they showed disrespect to the academic establishment by doubting such "assured results" of higher criticism as the post-Mosaicity of the Pentateuch, the mythical character of the early chapters of Genesis, the seventh-century date of Deuteronomy, the second-century date of Daniel, and the pseudonymity of Isaiah 40–66, the Fourth Gospel, the Pastorals, and 2 Peter. Second, evangelicals treated Jesus' demonstrable confidence in Scripture as decisive for their own and diagnosed Christians who disbelieved the Bible as disloyal to Christ. Third, they insisted that Christianity requires personal faith in Jesus Christ as one's prophet, priest, and king—an insistence constantly misheard as a demand for a stereotyped sudden conversion. It was on these rather wearisome conventionalities that Hebert, in the style of a genial veteran instructing the foolish young, had rung the changes.

My book, which begged that the word *fundamentalism* be dropped, the infallibility of Scripture recognized, and biblical evangelicalism acknowledged as mainstream Christianity, also said nothing that had not been said before. But, appearing at a time when British evangelicals were looking for ammunition, it was kindly received and widely read. It was published in America (though it was not addressed to the American scene, of which at that time I knew little) and it remains in print there; it has since 1996 been available again in Britain, where another book of mine, *God Has Spoken*, has long been making the same case in a less polemical and more pastoral way.

In the ongoing North American debate between evangelical and liberal Protestants, in which a large number of the former took the name "fundamentalists" as a badge of honor, signifying their stand for Christian fundamentals,[6] biblical inerrancy was from the first made the touchstone more directly and explicitly than was ever the case in the parallel debates in Britain.[7] This, I now think (I did not always think so), argues for clearer-sightedness in the New World, for without inerrancy the structure of biblical authority as evangelicals conceive it collapses.

Biblical authority means believing, affirming, applying, and obeying all biblical teaching, both informative and directive, and submitting all human opinion—worldly, churchly, and personal—to the judgment of that teaching. This procedure assumes that all biblical teaching is trustworthy truth from God. It would, after all, be a Hitlerish negating of our rational humanity to demand total acceptance of what is not totally true. But if Jesus Christ and his apostles are trustworthy teachers, the assumption is justified. For the New Testament documents put it beyond doubt, as a matter of history, that these teachers, the founders of Christianity, viewed all Scripture, as such, as God's abiding and reliable instruction, divinely authoritative against all human views that diverged from it.[8] The interpretation of it could be, and was, disputed at key points, but its inspiration could not. "The Scripture cannot be broken" (John 10:35). It is *inerrant*.

Inerrancy

Though *inerrancy*, like *Trinity*, is not a biblical word, it expresses a biblical thought. Inerrancy, meaning the full truth and trustworthiness of what the Bible tells us, is entailed, that is, necessarily and inescapably implied, by the God-givenness of what is written.

Certainly, the confession of inerrancy needs to be circumscribed by precise hermeneutical guidelines. What is inerrant is the expressed sense, the meaning that can be read out of the text in its own context; not any imposed sense, any meaning that can be read into the words when they are placed in a different context. Moreover, interpreters are not inerrant, and time-honored interpretations are not always beyond criticism.

Certainly, too, the confession of inerrancy requires clarity about the extent of the biblical canon. Only God-given Scripture, as such, is to be believed inerrant and treated as a sure rule for faith and life.

Also, the confession of inerrancy assumes awareness of

the radical incompetence of our fallen minds in matters theological. Only so will God's gift of the inerrant Book be properly valued, and only so will it be properly put to use as light for our path. Only so will the Adamic delusion that we can know better than the Word of God be seen for the irreverence and folly that it is, and only so shall we escape the related delusion that our right and duty to believe the Bible depends on our own ability to prove it true. The veracity of God, its primary author, is the warrant for our believing it: "it is to be received, because it is the Word of God."[9]

To disbelieve, and try to correct, any part of the Bible is always a recipe for some error about God and some ignorance of him as well as being a real if unintended insult to him. But those who heed the testimony of Christianity's founders to the spiritual blindness of fallen man will not lapse in this way.

Given all this, it is plain that the confession of inerrancy will, and should, function as a basic determinant of one's way of using the Bible. It prescribes the expository approach that seeks to see how one biblical passage fits with another—the approach that has been called *the analogy of Scripture*, and *the analogy of faith*. It forbids all modes of opposing Scripture to Scripture, of positing real discrepancy and self-contradiction within Scripture, and thus, as it is sometimes put, of "criticizing the Bible by the Bible." It requires that God be kept in view as the narrator of the history, the preacher of the sermons, the teacher of the wisdom, and the deviser of the worship forms (prayer and praises) that Scripture sets before us. It requires that when the harmony and coherence of biblical statements escape us, we put this down to the inadequacy of our insight rather than the incompetence of God's penmen. Inerrancy thus goes far to settle the shape of one's biblical scholarship and the content of one's eventual beliefs. North American evangelicals as a body have seen this, and they have confessed accordingly.

The Wenham Conference

However, there are exceptions. And this explains why in 1966 I found myself in company with fifty scholars from ten countries at a ten-day private conference held in Wenham, Massachusetts. The conference was called in hope of healing a breach that had developed between some faculty members and trustees of Fuller Seminary and the rest of North America's evangelical academic world.[10] Fuller had been founded in 1947 with a view toward opening an era of triumphant antiliberal scholarship and standardizing a broadly Reformed theology filtered through an apologetic rationalism of a developed fundamentalist type. Fundamentalism had by now become a defensive mindset, prone to fit God into a ready-made conceptual box and forget his transcendence and incomprehensibility.

Fuller had recruited teachers who, reacting against what they saw as simplistic one-sidedness in their own fundamentalist upbringing, now declined to affirm the full truth of Scripture. Their reasons varied. Three scholars (two of whom were at the Wenham conference) appeared to hold, on the basis of observing the "phenomena" of the text, that some statements in Scripture on matters of historical, geographical, and scientific detail are evidently "nonrevelational," and of these some are equally evidently wrong.[11] Another scholar (not at Wenham) seemed to think that the conceptual inadequacies of some parts of Scripture constitute mistaken assertions. Another seemed to decline the word *inerrancy* because it was associated with an inferior style of interpretation. Those who organized and funded Wenham wanted it to be a peace conference, either resolving the differences or showing that all were already agreed deep down. But all were not agreed, and peace was impossible, although a friendly communique was issued at the end. Division continued.[12]

The International Council on Biblical Inerrancy

In 1977, concern over growing uncertainty among evangelicals regarding Scripture led to the formation of the International Council on Biblical Inerrancy (ICBI), on which I was privileged to serve under the vigorous chairmanship of James M. Boice. (Living in England at that time, I was in fact the entire reason for "International" since all other Council members were Americans living in the U.S.A.) The council announced "as its purpose the defense and application of the doctrine of biblical inerrancy as an essential element for the authority of Scripture and a necessity for the health of the church. It was created to counter the drift from this important doctrinal foundation by significant segments of evangelicalism and the outright denial of it by other church movements."[13]

Over its ten-year life the ICBI mounted three "summits" for scholars and leaders, dealing respectively with the meaning of inerrancy, the principles and practice of biblical hermeneutics, and the application of a trusted Bible to key problems of personal and community life. It also held two major congresses on biblical faith and life today and produced or sponsored a series of substantial books, besides its *Foundation Series* of dignified tracts.[14] (See also pp. 124-25.)

To round off the ICBI story, I move for a moment two years beyond my announced terminus, to 1987. In that year the council closed down, believing that for the present its work was done. What had been accomplished? In the words of Dr. James Boice: "The literature produced by ICBI has been disseminated round the world; similar supportive organizations have been founded; and the three 'Affirmation and Denial' statements have achieved almost creedal stature in some quarters. The Council believes that many have been recalled to the highest standards of biblical authority by these efforts."[15] I think this is so. By God's grace, the inerrancy line was held and its strategic significance was made plain. Worthwhile new work expounding, vindicating, and applying it was done. A far higher degree of consensus than could have been anticipated was achieved on difficult questions of interpreting and applying Scripture. And the model of noninerrantist evangelicalism that, until recently at any rate, remained part of Fuller Seminary's stock in trade, was made to appear more than a little eccentric and unfruitful.[16] I continue to thank God as I remember ICBI.

The Evangelical Resurgence

But back now to things that happened before 1985. So far

from standing alone, or being a pioneer, ICBI was from the first carried along on the crest of a large-scale wave of evangelical resurgence. This in its academic expression was under way on both sides of the Atlantic well before 1955, seeking not just to defend the faith but to recapture the theological initiative that had been lost through liberal capture of the major church establishments.

In Britain the resurgence effectively began with the founding in 1938 of the Biblical Research Committee, later the Tyndale Fellowship, within the network of the Inter-Varsity Christian Fellowship (now Universities and Colleges Christian Fellowship) in order to nurture evangelical scholars and foster evangelical biblical scholarship.[17] Now possessed of a superb research library (Tyndale House, Cambridge) and a first-class academic journal *Tyndale Bulletin,* currently published twice yearly), the Tyndale Fellowship has seen more than two dozen of its members teach theology in British research universities, over and above the far larger number who have held positions in Britain's graduate theological colleges.

In the United States, B. B. Warfield (d. 1921), J. Gresham Machen (d. 1937) and his successor at Westminster Seminary, Ned B. Stonehouse (d. 1962), had maintained a pattern of constructive academic interaction at a technical level with nonevangelical specialists in their fields. But it was the founding of Fuller Seminary in 1947 that marked the moment when the thought of a crusading counterattack on entrenched liberalism effectively took hold of American evangelical minds.[18] (It was only in the 1960s that this vision seemed to be lost at Fuller; I continue to hope it is in process of being regained.) Manpower for this new era of biblical scholarship soon emerged through the growth of the evangelical student movement in the 1950s, followed by the Jesus movement of the next decade. The fallout from all this remains impressive enough to lead Richard Lovelace (and latterly, John White) to allege that a revival is now in process.[19] The remarkable expansion of the evangelical seminary world during this fifty-year period has meant more posts for evangelical scholars and a corresponding increase in the output of literature elucidating the Bible as the Word of God and countering the erratic skepticism of liberal Bible work. A study of publishers' catalogs over the past generation tells the tale.

Writing in 1985, Mark Noll gave details of "the profusion of outstanding commentaries . . . four academic series . . . six other semi-popular series . . . general dictionaries of theology, Christian ethics, and church history . . . several large introductions to the discussion of criticism as applied to both the Old and New Testaments . . . Bible translations . . . the fruit of an academic rebirth."[20] In these enterprises, as Noll points out, British scholars led at first, but their American colleagues are currently overtaking them, and Australian and Asian contributors to the mix have also appeared.

The reality of academic recovery, consolidation, and staying power appears from many facts: the steady flow of critical[21] and elucidatory books on the Bible from sizable firms like Eerdmans, Word, Baker, Zondervan, and the InterVarsity presses of Britain and the United States; the emergence of a small fleet of evangelical technical journals, with Britain's *Tyndale Bulletin* as its flagship; the seminal influence of the quiet Scottish commentator, historian, and textbook author F. F. Bruce, who supervised a record number of doctoral theses on biblical themes written by American scholars; the vigor of Britain's Tyndale Fellowship and America's own Evangelical Theological Society (founded in 1949, now over 2,000 strong) and Institute for Biblical Research (created in 1970 for specialists and boasting a current membership of 150); the blossoming among evangelicals of "biblical theology," understood as the unfolding of the progress of the historical-redemptive biblical message according to the analogy of faith,[22] a discipline notably pioneered and programmed by Edmund Clowney;[23] Westminster Seminary's doctoral program in hermeneutics, which President Clowney saw into place, and parallel endeavors in other places; and the observable process whereby, while the number of veteran evangelical scholars grows steadily, leadership in the biblical fields, as elsewhere, increasingly passes to younger men. The advance since 1955 has been spectacular. Resurgent evangelical biblical scholarship has come to stay.

The purpose of academic biblical study in any age is that the Word of God may be preached and heard within the frame and mindset of that age—challenging it, no doubt, but first tuning into it. The necessary disciplines are *linguistic,* for fixing the meaning of the Hebrew and Greek sentences; *literary* and *historical,* for focusing the message that each biblical book and each unit within each biblical book was conveying to its intended readership; *theological,* for integrating the various messages into the total frame of God's historical self-disclosure; *hermeneutical,* for transposing biblical teaching into different cultures without loss and seeing how it should shape service of God in our world today; and *homiletical*, for hammering home the awareness that God's Word to the world in Scripture is personally addressed to every individual whom it reaches.

It is by blessing the practice of these disciplines, at whatever level each Bible student operates, that the Spirit interprets the Word. The true goal of biblical scholarship is to present an adequately interpreted Bible to preachers and Bible students—and so to the whole church. At this point the resurgent evangelical biblical scholarship is essentially traditional in both its method and its findings. Its own detailed technical work leads it so to be and take its stand on essentials in the places where conservative Protestants have been standing ever since the Reformation. Advanced academic technique has confirmed the rightness of continuity with the evangelical past, rather than encouraging novelty of belief. The militant conservationism in theology that marks mainstream evangelicals reflects their certainty that, given a trusted Bible to be expounded as a whole in its own terms, the key features of Christianity—the divine triunity; human fallenness; incarnation; reconciliation; new creation; faith, hope, love—are found to be unambiguously plain and have, in fact, been found so for centuries. At the present juncture in Christian history, what is needed is not novelty, but a renewal of this heritage through a return to its biblical roots—and, thank God, this is what seems to be taking place in the evangelical world.

Nonevangelical Perspectives

Among nonevangelical Protestants, however, the story is different, though the goal of giving an interpreted Bible to preachers and to the whole church is formally the same. In these circles Scripture is seen as no more than human witness to God—uneven, fallible, and sometimes wrong—and this inevitably affects theological method in drastic ways. For many years, "critical" biblical scholarship (as nonevangelical study of Scripture proudly called itself) made little of the theological, hermeneutical, and homiletical disciplines and treated the deliverances of historical exegesis (i.e., "what it all *meant*") as the whole of biblical interpretation. Our fifty-year period, however, saw several endeavors against a "critical" background to recover the missing dimensions of interpretation, through which knowledge of the original significance might be made to show how life should be lived here and now (i.e., "what it all *means*"). The three such endeavors that seem to have been most influential will now be reviewed.

Interpretation according to "biblical theology." In the 1940s and 1950s, when I was in the process of my own theological formation, the movement in the world of "critical" study that took to itself the name "biblical theology" (not, as we shall see, in quite the same sense in which modern inerrantists use the phrase) was riding high. It was, however, riding for a fall. This movement had broken surface in Britain in the work of such scholars as Sir Edwyn Hoskyns, Gabriel Hebert, H. H. Rowley, Alan Richardson, and A. M. Hunter; in the United States in the writings of such as G. Ernest Wright, Floyd V. Filson, James D. Smart, Krister Stendahl, Paul Minear, Millar Burrows, and Bernhard W. Anderson.[24]

The academic aim of this movement was to understand

the Scriptures in terms of their contents; its churchly aim was to restore the sense that the Bible is revelation, a sense that two generations of criticism seemed to have effectively destroyed.[25] Its central idea was that, without jettisoning the "assured results" of higher criticism regarding the composition of biblical books and the true shape of Israel's history, the church should read the canonical Scriptures "from within," that is, as expressions of a faith and a hope in the living God that we in this latter day must re-appropriate. All Scripture, however uneven and unreliable in other respects, is a product of community faith in the almighty Creator-Redeemer, who finally and climactically made himself known in Jesus Christ. And no Scripture is properly understood save by coming to terms with that faith. It is profitless to know Bible history if one does not go on to grasp the truth about God that Bible history reveals. Joining hands at this point with the theology of the "neo-orthodox" pundit, Emil Brunner, which was also riding high in the fifties, "biblical theology" proclaimed itself the key to a renewing of personal faith and churchly consciousness, and so of corporate Christian life.

This approach led at once to a new seriousness in listening to the theology of the Bible's own theologians and in taking to heart what they most emphasized, namely, the soteriology and eschatology flowing from their belief that their gracious Creator had acted mightily for them in world history in the past and would in due course do so again. That was gain. But the movement had an Achilles' heel. It was trying to ride two horses, that is, to embrace the full biblical supernaturalism of theistic faith without letting go of the rationalistic and naturalistic antitheism of the Enlightenment, which had controlled the development of the "critical" movement from the first. Incoherence and confusion were the inevitable results.

Under interrogation, "biblical theology" proved unable to clear its mind as to whether it saw itself as studying God's self-revelation, which would of course be absolute and abiding truth, or simply the beliefs about God of certain Jewish and Christian writers. Beliefs about God, after all, however exalted and impressive in human terms, do not necessarily express absolute and abiding truth at all. It became apparent also that to gloss over this ambivalence the movement had developed another one—a form of double talk about God in history that carefully avoided implying anything about God's relation to the life we now live, since "God in history" meant no more than "Bible writers' idea of God in history" (an "idea" that might or might not be true).[26]

Homiletically, therefore, the sound and fury of all the talk about the mighty acts of God proved in the end to signify nothing. Also, in the interests of highlighting the distinctiveness of biblical material, exaggerated and simplistic claims were made about the theological unity of the two testaments, separately and together; about the characteristic uniqueness of Hebrew thought forms; and about the way word study illuminates the meaning of key Bible texts. When in due course it became clear that these claims were overblown, the movement's credibility was felt to be exploded.[27]

At this time, "biblical theology" is in eclipse.[28] "Critical" scholarship is currently preoccupied with the plurality and diversity of the Bible. Liberal churches generally have ceased to believe that any form of Bible-based renewal can help them. And evangelicals study the contents of Scripture on the basis that the text is God-breathed for our learning and that since its contents spring from one divine mind, its unity is a given starting point rather than a possibility to be debated. Falling between all three stools and with no one currently calling for its services, "biblical theology" as defined has no obvious future. Its legacy of theological dictionaries remains a valuable academic aid,[29] but its program for restoring the authority of a well-interpreted Bible to the church must be held to have failed. The movement itself is dying, if not dead.

A variant of the "biblical theology" approach, separately developed but similarly motivated, is "narrative theology," which focuses on the biblical accounts of God in action and draws its doctrine of how things are from the way God's story is told. This approach has spun off much vivid evangelistic and pastoral teaching about letting our personal story become part of God's story, and has prompted much useful thought on how God involves us humans in his story and leads us into a life of Jesus-likeness thereby. But, like "biblical theology," it cannot tell us whether biblical narratives are true or whether the Christ of the Bible is real, so that the skill of its exponents in highlighting the beliefs about God that the stories embody finally goes for nothing.

Scottish paper money is not accepted in England, nor are Canadian dollar bills accepted in the U.S.A.; in each case a currency change is necessary. In the same way, when the insights of "biblical theology" and "narrative theology" are expressed in inerrantist currency they become valuable aids to grasping the scriptural witness to the living God. As systems alternative to the evangelical view and use of Scripture, both fail; as resources for enriching that view, however, each has helpful specifics to offer. But the Bible will not be known as the living Word of the living God till the mainstream understanding of biblical authority takes hold once more of Christian minds.

Interpretation according to Karl Barth. To say that Barth (1886-1968) aimed to give the Bible back to the church would be true, but it would not be the whole truth. Barth was a brilliant and powerful systematic theologian whose goal, like that of the Reformers four centuries before him, was to give Christianity itself back to a church that had largely lost it. For more than a century theologians with the mindset of the Enlightenment in the various Protestant churches had been relativizing Christian faith and morals to the ongoing flow of secular culture. Barth sought to reverse this by setting forth the self-authenticating witness of a self-authenticating Bible to the self-authenticating risen Christ. This Christ, Barth argued, is present with us through the Spirit as one who by his death and resurrection has already reconciled our sinful race to our Maker.

In his unfinished *Church Dogmatics,* written on the grandest scale (six million words!), Barth's constant theme was the sovereign freedom and amazing grace of God in Jesus Christ. It is Christ who is the incarnate Word of divine self-revelation, whom all Scripture attests as the source, focus, and goal of everything that is. Barth's plan was to offer a version of mainstream Christianity—trinitarian, incarnational, redemptive—that would checkmate the Enlightenment's confidence in reason by being drawn

wholly from Scripture and being methodologically imper-
vious to any form of rationalistic criticism. He dismissed as
invalid, irrelevant, and irreverent all natural theology and
apologetics, both Roman Catholic and Protestant, all
claims that historical criticism deepens insight into the real
meaning of the Bible, and all ideas of agreements with
non-Christian religions.

Barth set himself to draw our entire knowledge of God
from narratives in Scripture that show him in action, par-
ticularly from the gospel story of the incarnate Word and
primarily within that story from Good Friday, Easter, and
Pentecost—the three supreme moments in the incarnate
Word's existence. To all of this, on Barth's view, the New
Testament witnesses historically in retrospect, and the Old
Testament typologically in anticipation.

So far, so good, one might think. But in Barth's working
out of his agenda, in which everything depended on how
convincingly he handled the Bible, two major problems
emerged.

First, Barth would not affirm the God-givenness of the
biblical text as a divine-human product—God's instruc-
tional witness to himself in the form of celebratory and
didactic human witness to him. Barth saw, no doubt, that
such an affirmation would require him to maintain the
inerrancy of Scripture, and he shied away from that.[30] Instead, he construed the inspiration of the text in terms of its
instrumentality in God's hands as his means of channeling
to us his specific word of the moment, thus causing the
written text to *become* the Word of God to us. That God uses
Scripture in this way is an important truth in bibliology,
and Barth does well to highlight it. But when he catego-

rizes the text as fallible, inadequate human witness that God honors by speaking through it, Barth drastically loosens the link between what the human writer was expressing and what God means us to learn at this moment from the passage in its canonical context.

Barth's approach opens the door to fanciful typology while closing it to any treatment of recorded divine commands as universal directives to be applied by systematic moral reasoning. These are daunting features of his position. Barth's theological exegesis of the most general of biblical imperatives yields only indicatives, not imperatives, because his method requires him to treat the texts as human testimony to what God once said rather than as God's direct indication to all readers concerning his moral will. Barth's ethics prove to be a kind of situationism, or contextualism,[31] whereby moral priorities are discerned through knowledge of the specific acts in which God's purposes were revealed. Surely something has been lost here.

Second, the attempt to support Barthian distinctives by straightforward biblical exposition repeatedly fails. Barth's negating of general revelation as a basis for natural theology; his insistence on the priority of Christ to Adam and of gospel to law (with the supralapsarianism, that is, the view that God directly willed the fall, that this involves); and his universalistic claim that all mankind, having been rejected in Christ's death, was then elected in Christ's resurrection (a claim that makes the non-salvation of anyone at all an apparent impossibility, as Barth acknowledged)—none of these can be made good by any ordinary form of exegesis. Specific texts stand against them, and Barth's speculative typology proves nothing.[32]

Barth's work over half a century has certainly renewed in some quarters a sense that we must go to the Bible for God's message. But it can hardly be said to have given the Bible back to the preacher and the church as a revitalizing force. Certain of Barth's characteristics had a significant impact on the church: the novelty of his exegesis, which makes ingenuity seem more important than fidelity to the text in its context; the almost hypnotic elegance of Barth's formulations, which leaves one feeling that any theology would do, provided it was beautiful; and Barth's paradoxical use of our down-to-earth Bible to construct an abstract and seemingly non-historical scheme of conceptual Christocentrism, which, as R. H. Roberts puts it, "hovers above us like a cathedral resting upon a cloud, structurally detached from space-time reality."[33] These unique characteristics have spawned in today's church an uncontrolled and currently uncontrollable theological pluralism based on selective and fanciful use of biblical material by each thinker. This pluralism, more than anything else, is Barth's actual legacy to us. His theology will undoubtedly be the subject of much academic study for many years. But his adventurous expositions of Scripture, throughout *Church Dogmatics* and elsewhere, will ultimately, I think, be rated as experiments that failed in the end to cast much light on the message of the text.

Interpretation according to Rudolf Bultmann. Bultmann of Marburg, Barth's contemporary, who died in 1976 at the age of 92, was another theologian who sought to give the Bible back to the preacher. But whereas Barth's way of doing this was by Christocentric exposition, Bultmann's was by radical "demythologization." In addition to being a skilled New Testament exegete and critic, Bultmann was also a Heideggerian existentialist who insisted, on the basis apparently of the Kantian distinction between the *phenomenal* and *noumenal* realms brought up to date, that God cannot be an object of knowledge as "worldly" realities are. He hit the headlines by dismissing all New Testament affirmations about the words and deeds of God as *myth,* that is, a prescientific way of conceiving reality that is simply not open to twentieth-century Westerners. Myth may inform us about the person who utters it, but not about anything else.

Bultmann assumed that we must, and do, treat science as our sole source of knowledge about the external world. So all those formalized theological beliefs, which earlier generations thought that God himself had taught us, must be given up, and we must be clear that nothing really depends on knowing facts about Jesus. Yet, if we ask the New Testament texts to speak to us about our own *existence* (defining that word dynamically and activistically, as is the existentialist way), they will do for us what we and all humankind most need; that is, they will draw, nudge, drive, or lure us into a new view of ourselves, so that we become persons who are no longer in the power either of the remembered past, through guilt, or of the unknown future, through fear. This new "self-understanding," which thus brings freedom, is what the entire New Testament is about—and all that it is about.

The way into the new mentality is by *decision,* that is, by committing ourselves to embrace this new view of ourselves and live it out. And the benefit of the decision is conceived in existentialist terms: thus you achieve your authentic existence, which the New Testament calls eternal life. This, said Bultmann, speaking the language of what to him is New Testament myth, is our Easter, our co-resurrection with Christ (although, of course, there was for him no space-time bodily resurrection of Jesus). This is our new birth and our new creation (although, of course, there was for Bultmann no more to it than our own decision). The only real act of God anywhere, ever, that Bultmann allows is the impact of Christian preaching. This preaching, by highlighting our inward predicament of guilt and fear and calling on us to decide to leave it behind, triggers the self-understanding that transforms our lives. Thus, the preacher's task is to practice the discipline of demythologization, in which he constantly explains this new self-understanding (nothing more, nothing less, nothing different) as being the whole of New Testament Christianity, and he exhorts us not to look for more. Such must be his lifelong pulpit ministry.

The remarkable influence that Bultmann's hermeneutical reductionism[34] has had over the past half-century was due, no doubt, more to the academic brilliance of his various expositions and the filling of teaching posts in German universities with his technically well-qualified disciples than to any intrinsic wisdom or profundity in what he had to say. The gospel according to Bultmann is like the Cheshire cat's smile in Lewis Carroll's *Alice in Wonderland*, visible in the air after the cat had vanished. It is a phenomenon of reassurance, but there is really nothing there.

It seems clear that Bultmann's idiosyncratic star, which in 1955 seemed to have risen above Barth's, was by 1985 decisively on the wane; and it seems clear, too, that whatever else Bultmann has done, he has not given the Bible back to the preacher and the church in a way that can lead to new spiritual life.

Watchers of the professional theologians' world will note a striking and significant parallel between the way current Protestant theology has dealt with the Bible on the one hand and the person of Christ on the other. In both cases the split is between those who call themselves liberals and progressives because they embrace the man-centered, rationalistic, anti-supernatural, anti-traditional, evolutionary mindset of the European Enlightenment, and those whom I call conservationists, who think this progressivism a perversity and hold to the old paths.

Conservationist reflection on both the divine-human person of Jesus Christ and the divine-human text of Holy Scripture starts by affirming the reality of the divinity and then celebrates the exaltation of the humanity in union with it, whereas liberal reflection on both starts by emphasizing the limits of the humanity and ends up scaling the divinity down. Liberals have thus developed Christology "from below," viewing Jesus simply as a man through whom God showed something special, and bibliology "from below," presenting the Bible as fallible human narration and instruction through which God triggers attitudes of approval and endorsement, or of disapproval and adjustment, towards its contents. Conservationists think that this reductionism makes faith in Christ and in Scripture as modeled in the New Testament simply impossible. So the intellectual legacy of the Enlightenment has precipitated a battle for the Incarnation as well as for the Bible—one battle, in fact, in which the battle for the Bible has become part of the larger battle for the gospel.

Biblical theology, Barth, and Bultmann all fell short, in their different ways, through conceding to Enlightenment prejudice at vital points, and any future bibliology and Christology that makes such concessions will also likewise fail. In current culture the Enlightenment mindset, though sorely wounded by postmodernist reaction, is by no means dead, and it is certainly not dead yet in the world of Christian theology. So the battle for the Bible, the Incarnation, and the gospel must, it seems, continue for the foreseeable future.

Conclusions

My narrative has, I believe, hit the high spots of debate about the Bible in the West over the past half-century, and I now conclude it.[35] Surveying the story from the standpoint of the dual interest (academic and pastoral) I confessed at the outset, what are the appropriate comments to make on it? I offer the following.

First, a Bible that can be read and trusted by all Christians as straightforward instruction from God himself about his relation to his world and everything in it is a precious gift, one that the church and, indeed, the entire human race needs. Satanic strategy will certainly seek to obfuscate that instruction by one means or another through generating either some mistrust of the text or some mishandling of it in exposition. Our story bears witness particularly to the second type of obfuscation.

Second, we should be thankful to God both for the gift of

Scripture itself and for all efforts to uphold its status as an authority and a means of grace to God's people by vindicating its inerrancy and infallibility on the one hand and by expounding the salvation it sets forth in Christ on the other hand. We should see these two endeavors as going together—needing each other for fruitfulness to the church and suffering together if either is undermined or neglected.

Third, we must allow our principles of interpretation to be determined *a posteriori,* from within the canonical Scriptures themselves. Since each book was written to be understood by its own first readers, our understanding of it must start from what it was expressing to them; and since all the books turn out when analyzed to be dealing, one way or another, with the history and scope of God's salvation—past, present, and future—and to be confronting their readers with the God who saves, our understanding of them must center here. This means that grammatical-historical interpretation from a redemptive-historical perspective must ever be our method. Furthermore, if biblical passages are not identified within the canon as, for instance, myth or type, we should resist the temptation to treat them as such. Our task as interpreters is to read out of Scripture what is demonstrably there, not to read into it what is possibly not there. Type, to be sure, is a biblical category, but is myth? Though this is not the place to argue the point, let me say, I think not.

Fourth, we must not view the methodological diversity of interpretative styles and conclusions in the modern church as anything but a tragedy. The theological pluralism and confusion of our day argues weakness of the flesh rather than vitality of the heart. It is cause for thanksgiving that evangelical theology all over the world, working as it does with an agreed method, remains fairly homogeneous and, if anything, slowly becomes more so. This is how under God it should be, as the Spirit works through the Word, and it is a process that we should try to further. But critical and corrective dialogue with nonevangelical theologies, constructed by use of a partly false method (as they all are), will have to go on. No serious, permanent rapprochement can be considered, even where by a happy accident views on particular subjects coincide, as long as methods diverge.

Evangelical method with the Bible is part of evangelical loyalty to the Bible, just as evangelical loyalty to the Bible is part of evangelical loyalty to Christ. And until agreement reaches to method, the battle for the Bible in the pluralistic maelstrom of the Christian world today will have to be maintained. May God strengthen his servants to continue fighting the good fight.

Appendix: A Short Statement

1. God, who is Himself Truth and speaks truth only, has inspired Holy Scripture in order thereby to reveal Himself to lost mankind through Jesus Christ as Creator and Lord, Redeemer and Judge. Holy Scripture is God's witness to Himself.

2. Holy Scripture, being God's own Word, written by men prepared and superintended by His Spirit, is of infallible divine authority in all matters upon which it touches: it

is to be believed, as God's instruction, in all that it affirms; obeyed, as God's command, in all that it requires; embraced, as God's pledge, in all that it promises.

3. The Holy Spirit, its divine Author, both authenticates it to us by His inward witness and opens our minds to understand its meaning.

4. Being wholly and verbally God-given, Scripture is without error or fault in all its teaching, no less in what it states about God's acts in creation, about the events of world history, and about its own literary origins under God, than in its witness to God's saving grace in individual lives.

5. The authority of Scripture is inescapably impaired if this total divine inerrancy is in any way limited or disregarded, or made relative to a view of truth contrary to the Bible's own; and such lapses bring serious loss to both the individual and the Church.

From the International Council on Biblical Inerrancy, 1978

4

GIVE ME UNDERSTANDING
The Approach to Biblical Interpretation

You have heard of the battle for the Bible—who hasn't? You have read quite a lot about it in the earlier pages of this book. You know what it is about—whether I can be a faithful, obedient, consistent Christian if I let go the total truthfulness, that is, the *inerrancy,* of Holy Scripture. You know, I am sure, some of the history that lies behind today's doubts as to whether we can trust the Bible or not. You know that for more than three hundred years God-shrinkers have been at work in the churches of the Reformation, scaling down our Maker to the measure of man's mind and dissolving the biblical view of him as the Lord who reigns and speaks. You know that in the rationalistic eighteenth century, Kant, the fountainhead of most later philosophy, set the example of ignoring, as a matter of method, the possibility that Scripture is God's instruction to us, and you know that many leaders of Western thought followed in his footsteps like a flock of sheep. You know that in the nineteenth century, dominated as it was by evolutionary ideas, the Bible was regularly downgraded, as reflecting times when religious thought was crude and unreliable in comparison with later notions. You know how scholars have labored to sort out the facts of Old Testament history from the "fancies" of Old Testament narrative, and to find the "real Jesus" amid the supposed New Testament distortions of him. You know how men in the street have boldly backed their judgment on all sorts of things against the witness of the written Word. You know that in our disillusioned late-twentieth century people are skeptical of liberal optimism and can no longer believe that everything is getting better and everyone is growing wiser and science tells us all we need to know. But you know, too, that neither biblical scholars nor philosophers nor the great mass of ordinary people have returned to the older confidence in Scripture as the revealed Word of God, true and trustworthy because of its divine source and able to give us the basic certainties about life and death that we need. This belief has not been re-established, despite all the efforts of Christians—call them conservatives, evangelicals, fundamentalists, orthodox, as you will, the name does not matter—who have sought to recall the church from worldly doubt to true faith at this point. These facts, which form the background of the battle, must by now be very familiar.

How should we regard this ongoing battle? It is a complex affair, carried on nowadays more by guerilla tactics than by open frontal engagements. In some locations there continues a not-very-happy domestic debate among professed evangelicals as to whether or not we can keep in step with each other in proclaiming to the world and maintaining in our scholarship and ministerial training that Scripture is all true. My hope is that the fire which has caused the smoke here will prove to have been fueled by nothing more than attempts to avoid certain words ("inerrant," "error-free," and other such), plus experiments by a few scholars who, having tried out in print their ideas about the Bible, will abandon them once they appear nonviable. Meanwhile, elsewhere on the same battlefield, hand-to-hand combat has died down. There is a temporary standoff as various types of liberals, aware that ability, integrity, acuity and consistency are found in the evangelical camp, withdraw from the conflict and dig in for the defense and furtherance of their wayward opinions. Scholars with all kinds of ideas about the Bible's meaning and relevance are currently busy stating and defending their views, and what in the way of constructive discussion may lie beyond this preliminary entrenchment does not yet appear.

Because evangelicals today have watched so many lapse from thoroughgoing biblical faith, and because they see how much depends on whether the Bible can be trusted or not, and because so many vested interests, denominational and institutional, are involved in the discussion, feelings and fears often run high, and this could be dangerous in several ways. I focus now on just one of the dangers, that of so concentrating on the tactics of the battle as to forget the strategy of the campaign and the kind of victory that is needed.

When a battle is on, those involved tend to think exclusively of winning and to lose sight of the cause for which the battle is being fought. I recall the days when the Second World War was drawing to its end and Allied leaders began to say that, having won the war, our next and harder task was to win the peace. But not enough thought was given to winning the peace, and the record of events during the past fifty years shows that it was not won. In retrospect, it almost looks as if we forgot what we had been fighting for. I am afraid that something similar might happen in the battle for the Bible. So I shall now do what I can to ward off this danger, by asking you to raise your eyes above the battlefield and think about a series of strategic questions which pinpoint the significance of the debate for the theological and spiritual health of churches and Christians.

My questions were suggested to me by the psalmist's prayer: "Give me understanding, that I may keep thy law and observe it with my whole heart" (Ps. 119:34, RSV). I should like to dwell on these words a moment before we go further.

Word and Spirit

How well do you know Psalm 119? Those who are wise come to know it very well, for they constantly seek to pray it. Why? Because it is a model, giant-size (176 verses long, twice the length of any other psalm and ten to twenty times the length of most), of that on which the wise know their well-being depends—namely, attention to what God has said. The psalmist celebrates the gift of divine instruction as "a lamp to my feet and a light for my path" (v. 105), without which he would be in the dark and unable to find his way. He hails God's Word as the means whereby he comes to know, love, and serve the God who gave it, and he admits that he would in every sense be lost without it. His prayer for understanding springs from this admission, for he recognizes that to understand God's Word—which means, to understand his own existence in the light of God's Word—is to know the way of life. Lack of understanding of God's Word is itself a state of death. The wise identify. They see that the fear of the Lord which is the beginning of wisdom starts with the understanding that God alone can give. So they follow the psalmist in cleaving to God's Word and in asking its Author to interpret it to them in its bearing on their lives.

As writing, the psalm dazzles. It divides into twenty-two sections, each marked by a different letter of the Hebrew alphabet and each consisting of eight verses starting with that letter. All save one of its 176 verses refer in some way to what the psalmist variously calls God's *word, words, precepts, statutes, law, promise, testimonies* and *ordinances,* which spell out God's *ways* and his *righteousness,* i.e., his revealed will for man, and the fertility of thought with which changes are rung on the theme of response to what God has said is amazing. Psalm 119 is a very clever composition. Indeed, it is more than that. It is a transcript of 176 distinct moments of devotion to God, and as such it is awesomely poignant. One wonders how far this heroic combination of ardor and humility, resolution and dependence, trouble and triumph, distress at the ways of men and delight in the ways of God, was realized in the psalmist's own life (for psalmists, like other poets, may perhaps verbalize beyond their experience); one wonders if it has ever been fully realized save in the heart of our Lord Jesus Christ himself. Augustine's idea that the Psalms are essentially prayers of Jesus Christ is surely in place here. What this psalm shows us is the perfection of the perfect heart in its unwavering openness to all that God teaches in the Scriptures, and the Gospels show that our Master was mastered completely by what came to him from his Bible. So must we seek to be, for that is the way we are called to go. Jesus' disciples must be Scripture's pupils.

Psalm 119 is the Bible's own exposition, written in advance, of Paul's statement in 2 Timothy 3:16-17 that all Scripture, being inspired by God, is profitable "for teaching, for reproof, for correction, and for training in righteousness, that the man of God may be complete, equipped for every good work" (RSV); and Paul's statement is the Bible's own summary of what this psalm is showing us.

"Give me understanding," prays the psalmist. Under many kinds of pressure and in a turmoil of emotions he yet holds fast to the Word of the Lord and rests his hopes in the Lord of the Word. Distrusting himself and his own thoughts, however, he prays for understanding five times (vv. 34, 73, 125, 144, 169). He fears lest he should misconceive or misapply God's teaching, or narrow it unduly. He wants to comprehend its full range and thrust as it bears on his thoughts, purposes, attitudes, reactions, relationships, view of things and people; and he wants to comprehend it so that he may conform to it. "Give me understanding, *that I may keep thy law.*" Every day this should be your prayer, and mine too, for it is not enough for us to know the text of Scripture if we fail to understand it, so that we think we are living by it when we are not.

The New Testament identifies the ministry of interpretation and application for which the psalmist asks as the work of the Holy Spirit. The Spirit is "the anointing which . . . teaches you about everything" (1 John 2:27, RSV), using as his means of instruction—his textbook, one might say—the contents of the Old and New Testaments. Understanding comes from the Spirit through the Word; Word and Spirit belong together. In the historic Anglican Prayer Book, the prayer set for the second Sunday in Advent, based on Romans 15:4, reads:

> Blessed Lord, who hast caused all holy Scriptures to be written for our learning: Grant that we may in such wise hear them, read, mark, learn, and inwardly digest them, that by patience and comfort of thy holy Word, we may embrace and ever hold fast the blessed hope of everlasting life . . .

The prayer set for Pentecost reads:

> God, who as at this time didst teach the hearts of thy faithful people, by the sending to them the light of thy Holy Spirit: Grant us by the same Spirit to have a right judgment in all things, and evermore to rejoice in his holy comfort . . .

Each of these prayers completes the thought begun by the other, and both are needed to express the full truth about the teaching work of God. More of that later.

I turn now to the series of questions which the psalmist's

prayer suggests that we who battle for the Bible need to be asking ourselves.

Authority

First, *why does biblical trustworthiness, whether we call it infallibility or inerrancy, matter?* Why should it be thought important to fight for the total truth of the Bible? Some, of course, do not think it important, either because this is a belief they do not share, or because they do not regard others' disbelief of inerrancy as either dishonoring God or disadvantaging the disbelievers. I, however, am one of those who think this battle very important, and this is why: Biblical *veracity* and biblical *authority* are bound up together. Only truth can have final authority to determine belief and behavior, and Scripture cannot have such authority further than it is true. A factually and theologically untrustworthy Bible could still impress us as a presentation of religious experience and expertise, but clearly, if we cannot affirm its total truthfulness, we cannot claim that it is all God's testimony and teaching, given to control our convictions and conduct.

Here is a major issue for decision. There is really no disputing that Jesus Christ and his apostles, the founders of Christianity, held and taught that the Jewish Scriptures (our Old Testament) were God's witness to himself in the form of man's witness to him. There is no disputing that Jesus Christ, God's incarnate Son, viewed these Scriptures as his Father's Word (see how he quotes a narrative comment as the Creator's utterance in Matthew 19:5, citing Genesis 2:24); or that he quoted Scripture to repel Satan

(Matt. 4:3-11); or that he claimed to be fulfilling both the law and the prophets (Matt. 5:17); or that he ministered as a rabbi, that is, a Bible teacher, explaining the meaning of texts of which the divine truth and authority were not in doubt (Matt. 12:1-14, 22:23-40, etc.); or that he finally went to Jerusalem to be killed and, as he believed, to be raised to life again because this was the way Scripture said God's Messiah must go (Matt. 26:24, 52-56; Luke 18:31-33, 22:37, cf. 24:25-27, 44-47). Nor is there really any disputing (despite skeptical poses struck by some scholars) that "God raised him from the dead" (Acts 13:30), thereby vindicating all he had said and done as right—including the way he had understood, taught, and obeyed the Scriptures. So, too, it is clear that the apostles, like their Lord, saw the Scriptures as the God-given verbal embodiment of teaching from the Holy Spirit (2 Tim. 3:16-17; Acts 4:25, 28:25; Heb. 3:7, 10:15); and that they claimed, not merely that particular predictions were fulfilled in Christ (cf. Acts 3:22-24), but that all the Jewish Scriptures were written for Christians (cf. Rom. 15:4, 16:26; 1 Cor. 10:11; 2 Cor. 3:6-16; 1 Pet. 1:10-12; 2 Pet. 3:16); and that they took over the Old Testament (Septuagint version) for liturgical and homiletical use in the churches alongside their own teaching. For it is also clear that the apostles understood inspiration as the relationship whereby God speaks and teaches in and through human instruction which is given, explicitly or implicitly, in his name. They also saw their own teaching and writing as inspired in just the same sense in which the Old Testament was inspired (cf. 1 Cor. 2:12, 14:37; 1 John 4:6; etc.), so that the later conjoining of their official writing with the Old Testament to form the two-part Christian Bible was a natural and necessary step. None of this is open to serious doubt.

So the decision facing Christians today is simply: will we take our lead at this point from Jesus and the apostles? Will we let ourselves be guided by a Bible received as inspired and therefore wholly true (for God is not the author of untruths), or will we strike out, against our Lord and his most authoritative representatives, on a line of our own? If we do, we have already resolved in principle to be led not by the Bible as given, but by the Bible as we edit and reduce it. We are then likely to be found before long scaling down its mysteries (e.g., incarnation and atonement) and relativizing its absolutes (e.g., in sexual ethics) in the light of our own divergent ideas.

And in that case Psalm 119 will stand as an everlasting rebuke to us: for instead of doubting and discounting some things in his Bible, the psalmist prayed for understanding so that he might live by God's law ("law" here means not just commands, but all authoritative instruction that bears on living). This is the path of true reverence, true discipleship, and true enrichment. But once we entertain the needless and unproved, indeed unprovable, notion that Scripture cannot be fully trusted, that path is partly closed to us. Therefore it is important to maintain inerrancy and counter denials of it; for only so can we keep open the path of consistent submission to biblical authority and consistently concentrate on the true problem, that of gaining understanding without being entangled in the false question of how much of Scripture should we disbelieve. This brings us to our next subject.

Interpretation

My second question is: *Under what conditions can the Bible, viewed as inspired and infallible divine instruction, actually exert authority over us?* My answer is this: Scripture can only rule us so far as it is understood, and it is only understood so far as it is properly interpreted. A misinterpreted Bible is a misunderstood Bible, which will lead us out of God's way rather than in it. Interpretation must be right if biblical authority is to be real in our lives and in our churches. The point is obvious, but is not always stressed as it needs to be.

Have you ever noticed that we use the phrase "Word of God" in two senses? Sometimes we use it to mean the text of Scripture, as when we call printed Bibles copies of the Word of God. That is a natural usage, but not a strictly scriptural one. When the Bible uses "word of God" in revelatory contexts, it means God's message, either (as in the prophets) a particular occasional communication to some person or persons, or (as in the New Testament) the gospel, God's message to the world, or (as in Psalm 119) the total message of the Scriptures. The psalmist's Bible, it would seem, was the five books of Moses; ours is larger, but the principle that all the Bible's teaching must be received as the Word of God remains unchanged. My present point is that you can have the Word of God in the first sense (by possessing a Bible, and knowing something of its text) without having it in the second sense; that is, without having understanding. The psalmist asked God for understanding, and so should we, lest after vindicating Scripture as the written Word of God we should still fail, as we say, to "get the message."

Faultless formulas about biblical inspiration and authority do us no good while we misunderstand the Bible for whose supremacy we fight. The major differences between historic Protestants and Roman Catholics—papal authority, the presence and sacrifice of Christ in the mass, the form and credentials of the ordained ministry, the way of salvation by grace through faith—are rooted in differences of interpretation; so are the major cleavages between Christians of all persuasions and Jehovah's Witnesses, with their anti-Trinitarianism, their anticipations of Armageddon, and their legalistic doctrine of salvation. Yet these groups have historically maintained the inerrancy of Scripture (some Roman Catholics are slipping these days, but that is a detail) and have claimed that all their distinctives are Bible-based. You see, then, how important the issue of interpretation is.

Recently the more traditional guidance on biblical interpretation (well presented to us in such books as R. C. Sproul's *Knowing Scripture* and A. M. Stibbs's *Understanding God's Word*, published by American and British Inter-Varsity Press respectively) has been augmented by the academic discipline called *hermeneutics*. This covers more than principles for interpreting the text; it centers on the interpreting subjects, that is, the people doing the interpretation, and on the way they come to perceive and embrace what God is showing them in and through the text. It is an important field of inquiry, into which evangelicals do well to move, as indeed their scholars are already doing. The rest of my questions in this discourse are in fact hermeneutical. They will show you something of the perspectives that hermeneutical study opens up.

Obstacles

Here is my third question: *What are the obstacles to our understanding the Bible?* Obstacles, I suggest, can emerge at two points. The first has to do with the *rules we follow.*

A venerable but zany way to seek from Scripture understanding of God's will for you is the so-called *sortes biblicae* (biblical lots). What you do is prayerfully open your Bible at random to see what text catches your eye, or prayerfully pick out a text with a pin while your eyes are shut: both methods have been tried. Campbell Morgan used to tell of the man who followed this method with the King James Version and came up with "Judas went out and hanged himself." Finding these words unhelpful, he did it again and this time got "Go, and do thou likewise." In desperation he tried once more and this time the words that jumped at him were, "That thou doest, do quickly." Morgan's point (mine too) is that though this practice shows vast reverence for Scripture as God's means of communicating with us, it is of itself superstitious and wrongheaded, savoring more of magic or witchcraft than of true religion; it is precisely not understanding God's Word.

Similar is the approach which detaches texts from their context to find personal meaning in them by feeding them into the world of one's private preoccupations and letting that world impose new senses on old phrases. Seventy years ago a theological student, who later became a close and valued friend, had committed himself to start his ministry in a church in the north of England when he received a very attractive invitation to join instead a teaching institution in South Wales. He did not feel able to withdraw from his commitment, but one day he read in Isaiah 43:6 (KJV) the words, "I will say to the north, Give up," and concluded that this was God telling him that he would be providentially released from his promise and so set free to accept the second invitation. No such thing happened, however, so he went north after all, wondering what had gone wrong. Then he reread Isaiah 43:6, and noticed that it continued, " . . . and to the south, Keep not back"! At this point it dawned on him that he had been finding in the text a meaning that was never really there, but had been reflected onto it by the concerns which he brought to his reading of it. To impose meaning on the text is not, however, the way to learn God's law. Yet we constantly do this—don't we?—and it is one chronic obstacle to understanding.

Rules of interpretation. There are basically three rules of interpretation. *First,* interpret Scripture *historically,* in terms of what each writer meant his own first readers to gather from his words. This means seeing each book in its own historical and cultural setting, and putting ourselves in both the writer's and the readers' shoes. Each book was written as a message to the writer's contemporaries, and only as we see what it was meant to tell them shall we discern what it has to say to us. The way into the mind of the Holy Spirit is through the meaning expressed by those whose thoughts and words the Spirit inspired.

Second, interpret Scripture *organically,* as a complex unity proceeding from one mind, that of God the Spirit, the primary author *(auctor primarius)* of it all. A simple human example will show what this means. The late C. S. Lewis was a virtuoso author who wrote criticism, literary history, philology, theology, apologetics, an allegory, poems, novels, and fantasies for both adults and children, yet who expressed a consistent Christian viewpoint in all his varied output. If you were studying Lewis, you would look beyond the formal differences between one of his books and another to focus on their common outlook. So with the sixty-six books of Holy Scripture. Holy Scripture is a library of great literary diversity to which more than forty writers contributed over more than a thousand years. They too, however, express one mind, the mind of their divine source. This appears from the demonstrable fact that they tell one story about one God, one Savior, one covenant, and one church, and teach one way of serving God, the way of faith, hope, and love, of repentance, obedience, praise, prayer, work, and joy. Following academic fashion, today's scholars concentrate on drawing contrasts, real and fancied, between one Bible writer and another, but practical Christians know that it is more fruitful to investigate how these writers blend. Scripture ought to be handled as an inspired organism of coherent truth, for that is what it really is.

Third, interpret Scripture *practically,* which means (to use a precise technical term) *dialogically*—seeking always the word God addresses to you, here and now, to prompt your response to him. In Bible study we start as flies on the wall, watching God deal with people of the past, overhearing his words to them and theirs to him, noting the outcome of their faithful or faithless living. But then we realize that the God whom we were watching is watching us, and that we too are wholly in his hands, and that we are no less called and claimed by him than were the Bible characters. Thus we move into dialogical interpretation. Having seen what the text meant for its writer and first readers, we now see what it means for us. We study Scripture in the presence of the living God, as those who stand under both it and him. Each time it is as if he has handed us a letter from himself and stays with us while we read it to hear what our answer will be. To have this awareness, and to pray, "Give me understanding, that I may keep thy law," and then to read Scripture (or hear it preached or read expositions of it) expecting Father, Son, and Spirit to meet, teach, question, challenge, humble, heal, forgive, strengthen, and restore you as you do so, is the crucial step in interpretation, to which historical and organic study are the preliminaries. In the preface to his first published volume of sermons, John Wesley formulated it thus:

> I am a creature of a day. . . . I want to know one thing, the way to heaven. . . . God himself has condescended to teach the way. . . . He has written it down in a book. O give me that book: At any price give me the book of God! I have it: here is knowledge enough for me. . . . I sit down alone: only God is here. In his presence I open, I read his book; for this end, to find the way to heaven. . . . Does anything appear dark and intricate? I lift up my heart to the Father of Lights. . . . I then search after and consider parallel passages. . . . I meditate thereon. . . . If any doubt still remain, I consult those who are experienced in the things of God: and then the writings whereby, being dead, they yet speak. And what I thus learn, that I teach.

Apart from the seeming narrowness of the phrase "way to heaven," which could divert concern from creative work for God on earth (though it did not so divert Wesley himself!), you could hardly spell it out more right-mindedly than that.

Pitfalls for the unwary. But now there is a second point at which obstacles to understanding arise, no matter how diligently we follow the rules. This has to do with *the blinkers we wear* (or *blinders,* as North Americans say).

You know what blinkers (blinders) are. They are the leather pads put over the eyes of street horses in the old days when carts and buses were horse-drawn, so that the animals could only see a little of what was in front of them. The blinkers narrowed their field of vision drastically, thereby keeping them from being startled by what they would otherwise have noticed happening around them. Skittish racehorses are blinkered on the track today for the same reason. Similarly, blinkering may operate in our minds as we study Scripture; wearing the blinkers may well keep us quiet, but only by keeping us from seeing what in fact we need to see. Let me show you what I mean.

You and I, like everyone else, are children of traditions, and hence are both their beneficiaries and their victims. They have opened our eyes to some things, and closed them to others. Most of us, I imagine, are children of Protestant, evangelical, pietist traditions in the different denominational families, Lutheran, Reformed, Presbyterian, Anglican, Brethren, Baptist, Methodist, Mennonite, Bible Church, or whatever. If we were reared Roman Catholic or Orthodox, the different traditions there will have left us different animals at some points from our Protestant brothers and sisters. The dispensational, pentecostal, covenantal, liberal, and other traditions of Bible teaching to which we have been exposed will also have made their mark, as will the inclusivist or separatist, large-group or small-group, institutionalized or free-style traditions of churchmanship to which we personally owe most allegiance. Being human, we shall see quite quickly how this shaping by environment applies to others at points where they differ from us and be very slow to see that it applies just as much to us, too. We have benefited from the traditions of our nurture and should be grateful. But we need to be aware that all traditions function as blinkers, focusing our vision on some things at which we have been taught to look constantly and which we therefore see clearly, but keeping us from seeing other things which other traditions grasp better.

Again: we are children, and therefore victims, of reaction—negative stances of recoil blinding us to the value in the things we reject. Human reaction never results in God's righteousness; it is not discerning enough. Thus, many Protestants have so reacted against Roman Catholic sacramentalism as to mistrust the sacraments entirely and in practice to deny their importance. (You could not guess from watching some churches that regular sharing in the Lord's Supper was prescribed by our Lord for his remembrance.) Other Protestants, by contrast, have so reacted against the anti-sacramentalism of their upbringing as to leave the Protestant fold entirely. Reaction against the formalism and aestheticism into which "liturgical" churches can lapse has led some to oppose all "set" prayers and all efforts toward dignity in worship, just as reaction against sloppiness and disorder in nonliturgical services has led others to turn their backs on spontaneity in worship altogether. Reaction against dry and heavy theology has made some of us woolly and wild, valuing feelings above truth, depreciating "head knowledge" by comparison with "heart knowledge" and refusing to allow that we cannot have the latter without the former, just as reaction against overheated emotionalism has made others of us cool, cerebral, and censorious to a fault. Reacting against yesterday's legalistic prohibitions regarding tobacco, alcohol, reading matter, public entertainment, dress, cosmetics, and the like, we have become licentious and self-indulgent, unable to see that the summons to separation and cross-bearing has anything to say to us at all. Sharing the reaction of our times against the past (we think of history as bunk, and of the latest word as necessarily the wisest), we cut ourselves off from our Christian heritage and end up rootless and unstable. These are just a few examples of how reaction, like tradition, can become a blinkering force, keeping us from seeing the value of sacraments, liturgy, theology, discipline, church history, and so on.

I am talking about what sociologists call *cultural prejudice*. I am saying that we all suffer from it, most of all those of us who think we don't, and that as a result we are constantly missing things that are there for us in the Bible. We are ourselves part of the problem of understanding because of the way that tradition and reaction have conditioned us. When, therefore, we ask God to give us understanding we should be asking him to keep us not only from mistakes about the meaning of texts but also from culturally determined blind spots. We cannot hope in this world to lose our blinkers entirely; we shall always be men and women of our time, nurtured by our cultural milieu and also narrowed by it. That is the inescapable human condition. But we can at least be aware of the problem, and try to surmount it as far as possible.

Understanding

I can now pose my fourth question, which you might have expected to be my first, but I had to work up to it. *What is meant by "understanding"?* What is the nature of the understanding for which we should pray?

I have already hinted at my answer; now, to crystallize it, I offer you two pictures. *First,* picture a *seminar,* as it might be conducted in universities known to me, and as I might try to conduct it myself in the college where I teach. There is a handful of students, all of whom are supposed to have done some reading on the day's topic, and one of whom has written an essay on it. The teacher has him or her read it to the class. Then there are two ways the teacher can go. He may choose to get the whole class dialoguing about the essay straight away. Or he may elect to dialogue himself with the essayist before that happens, filling in perspectives and, perhaps, giving some of his own reactions to what he has heard. Now imagine a seminar in which the instructor, himself an authority on the subject, is following the second course and doing it so skillfully that you, a member of the class, can see at once from his comments on the essay what he would have to say about your present ideas on the subject. By his direct dealing with the essayist, therefore, he is actually teaching you a great deal; should the seminar end without you speaking a word to him or him to you, you will still go out wiser than you came in. This illustrates what I earlier pictured as our fly-on-the-wall relationship to God's dealing with Bible characters and his address in and through the biblical books to their original recipients. By observing and overhearing we learn what God thought of their attitudes, assumptions, ambitions, and activities, and what changes in their mindset and lifestyle he wanted to see. This shows us what he must think of us and what changes he must want to see in us. That is understanding.

Second, imagine yourself being *coached* at tennis. If the coach knows his stuff, you are likely to experience him as a perfect pest. You make strokes as you have done for years, the natural, comfortable way. He interrupts: "Hey, not like that; that's no good; do it this way instead." If you say: "But I like doing it the way I did it, and it sometimes comes off, doesn't it?" the reply is: "Doing it your way you can't improve; it's a bad habit, and you must break it." The coach will readily explain why you have to change; what he will not do is let you go on as you are going. He works for your good, forcing you to step up your game, and in your sober moments you are grateful. But he makes such a nuisance of himself that often you wish he would go and jump in the lake! This illustrates the fact that understanding is never abstract and theoretical; it is always understanding of the work and will of the living God who constantly demands to change us. What is understood is ultimately God's claim on and purpose for our lives in light of all that he gives us in creation, providence, and saving grace. Notions about God's ways that carry no implications about our ways are not signs of understanding. Understanding, when given, is not always immediately welcome, for as W. H. Auden said in an appalling line—appalling not as poetry, but as stating something that is dreadfully true—"we would rather be ruined than changed." But God keeps at us!—and when, with the psalmist, we set ourselves to keep his law by grace and make such changes as he requires, we know the benefit.

The understanding, then, of which the psalmist speaks is a matter of receiving that *teaching* (first illustration) and that *reproof* and *correction* that leads to *training in righteousness* (second illustration) for which Paul said Scripture was *profitable* (2 Tim. 3:16). It means knowing what God's truth requires today in one's life. Such understanding does not come by mother wit, but is the gift of God.

Spirit and Understanding

This leads to my last question: *How does God give understanding?*

In Ephesians 3:16-19 Paul prays that "according to the riches of his glory [God the Father] may grant you to be strengthened with might through his Spirit in the inner man, and that Christ may dwell in your hearts through faith; that you, being rooted and grounded in love, may have power to comprehend with all the saints what is the breadth and length and height and depth, and to know the love of Christ which surpasses knowledge, that you may be filled with all the fullness of God" (RSV). From this breathtaking prayer I draw the following answer to my question. God gives knowledge (= understanding, cf.

Eph. 1:17-18; Col. 1:9; understanding in this case of Christ's love and how to respond to it): (1) through the Holy Spirit ("strengthened . . . through his Spirit," v. 16); and (2) through the Christian community ("with all the saints," v. 18). Let me develop these points.

God gives understanding through the Holy Spirit. This learning through the Holy Spirit does not cancel the need for study, any more than it invalidates the rules of interpretation which we spelled out earlier. Never oppose the work of the Spirit giving understanding to your work as a student seeking it; the Spirit works through our diligence, not our laziness. As we saw earlier, understanding of what God's written Word means for us comes through seeing what it meant when first put on paper, and applying that to ourselves. It is in application specifically that we need divine help. Bible commentaries, Bible classes, Bible lectures and courses, plus the church's regular expository ministry, can give us fair certainty as to what Scripture meant (and we should make full use of them to that end), but only through the Spirit's illumination shall we be able to see how the teaching applies to us in our own situation.

So, we should look not only to the commentators for the exegesis but also to the Spirit for the application, and to that end I commend to you three questions which you should constantly be asking as you read and weigh the sacred text. One: What does this passage tell me about *God*—his character, power, and purpose; his work, will, and ways in creation, providence, and grace? Two: What does this passage tell me about *man*—the human situation, humankind's possibilities, privileges, and problems, right and wrong ways of living, people in sin and people in grace? Three: What is all this showing me and saying to me about *myself* and my own life? Lift your heart to God and ask for the Spirit's help as you work through these three questions in the divine presence, and you will certainly be given understanding.

God gives understanding through the Christian community. Understanding does not usually, and certainly not fully, occur outside the fellowship of faith. This aspect of the matter is not stressed in Psalm 119, but Paul's words, "with all the saints," point to it, as does his directive in Colossians 3:16: "Let the word of Christ dwell in you richly as you teach and admonish one another with all wisdom, and as you sing psalms, hymns and spiritual songs with gratitude in your hearts to God." Only as we gratefully share with others what we know and receive from them what they know, will the "word of Christ" (the Christian message) dwell in us *richly* (abundantly and enrichingly), in the way that produces *wisdom.* Many of us are at a disadvantage here; we have had it so drummed into us that the only sure way to learn God's will from the Bible is to go off with it into a solitary place and dig into it on our own that we cannot easily accept that the interchanges of church fellowship, both institutional and informal, are the main channels of entry into spiritual understanding. But, though personal Bible reading is important for getting to know the text and is the duty as well as the privilege of all literate persons, Scripture shows that the main means of learning from God is to hear his message preached and to involve oneself in the give-and-take of Christian fellowship in exploring the contents of Holy Scripture.

Don't misread me! I do not question the value of the many excellent schemes of personal Bible study that are available today; nor do I question the profit of continuous private Bible reading, day in day out, something which I suspect most of us should be doing more than we are; nor do I forget that over and over again folk who had no biblical preaching within reach, nor any fellowship, have been wonderfully taught by God from Scripture alone. I am only saying that the New Testament expects that it is as we sit under the preaching and teaching of the Word and share with each other about it, rather than as we isolate ourselves to commune with the Bible as solitary individuals, that we shall be given understanding most fully (and have our offbeat ideas and blinkered prejudices corrected most speedily). Again, I do not forget that a Christian may not finally surrender his or her judgment to anyone; the responsibility which Paul imposed when he wrote, "test everything; hold fast what is good" (1 Thess. 5:21, RSV) remains, and I must constantly tell you, with reference to all the views I express here or anywhere else, "I speak to sensible people; judge for yourselves what I say" (1 Cor. 10:15). So now I ask you: Do I read the New Testament right? Is it not in company with the saints in the church, around and under the Word, that the apostles expect Christians to become adult in understanding? Please judge!

If so, what follows? *First,* that you and I should take most seriously the preaching under which we sit in our churches. We should pray for our preachers as they prepare, and for ourselves as we go to hear them, and we should listen not to criticize but to learn, even when the preacher is not one of the best. *Second,* we should take most seriously the value of group Bible study as a means to personal understanding and make a point of involving ourselves in it. *Third,* we should also take seriously the value of practicing fellowship with Christians outside our own circle by reading their books—including classic books from the Christian past and expository books written from standpoints other than our own within the Bible-believing spectrum. (Thus, for instance, Calvinists should sometimes read books by charismatics, and charismatics should sometimes read books by Calvinists.) This will help us get some of our blinkers off and see over the top of some of the ruts we are in.

The threefold benefit of correct understanding. Observing these maxims, and especially the third, will bring us a threefold benefit.

First, it will deliver us from the tyranny of *being tied to our own thoughts.* All our minds are narrower than we think, and blind spots and obsessions abound in them like bees in clover. Personal Bible study is always to some extent patchy and incomplete, for there is so much in each passage that we fail to see. We are unbalanced, too; those most interested in ideas focus on doctrine and forget ethics, those most interested in people focus on service and forget doctrine. We need the discipline of learning with the saints, past and present, in the ways noted above, to counterbalance our lopsidedness and to help us break out of the narrow circle of our own present thoughts into a larger vision and a riper wisdom.

Second, this procedure will deliver us from the tyranny of *being tied to our own time.* C. S. Lewis speaks of the "chronological snobbery" of those who care only to know the present because they think that only the present is worth knowing. Such snobbery is found in both the church and the world, and in both it is a naive cultural conceit which needs to be punctured. The best way to puncture it is to get back to the really big saints; reading the classics which in God's providence they left us will soon cut us down to size and bring us a great deal of ageless wisdom into the bargain. So (for instance) if you want to understand the dimensions of sin and grace, you really must read Augustine. If you want to get the measure of the world of faith, you really must read Calvin. If you want insight into the life of sanctification, you really must read the Puritans—Owen, Sibbes, Brooks, Gurnall, Bunyan, Baxter, and company. If you want to appreciate the height and might of God's work in revival, you really must read Jonathan Edwards. If you want to grasp what prayer is all about, you really must read folk like John of the Cross and that other giant of spirituality (for such he was), Martin Luther. The wisdom of these great souls finds us paddling in muddy shallows and takes us out to the deep things of God. It enlarges us spiritually as Sophocles, Shakespeare, and Dostoevsky enlarge us humanly. After every new book, urged C. S. Lewis, read two old ones. He meant two classics, and his advice was good. It is tyranny to be tied to one's own time and cut off from the wealth of the past—even if you are not conscious of it as tyranny. You and I will do well to break these bonds by keeping regular company with yesterday's great teachers.

Third, this procedure will deliver us from the tyranny of

being tied to our own heritage. As we saw, we are all children of tradition (that is, of a particular heritage of teaching and training), and it is certain that the tradition that shaped us had a narrowing as well as an enriching effect on us. But we can start to neutralize that narrowing effect by learning to appreciate traditions other than our own. Some assume that their own tradition is all right and anything that is in any way different must be all wrong. If you are assuming that, think again!—or rather, start thinking now, for it does not look as if you have thought seriously about it at all as yet. What do you expect of traditions? Do you think of them as all corrupt, and of yourself as untainted by them, or do you allow that there may be good in them, as for instance in the tradition (denominational, interdenominational, or whatever) which did most to shape your own present faith and life? The fact is that in each section of the church all over the world the tradition that has developed (teaching, worship patterns, hymns, style of nurture, etc.), whether viewed as definitive in the Roman Catholic and Orthodox manner or as merely provisional and pedagogic in the Protestant way, looks back to the Bible and offers itself as mediating the faith of the Bible. And since the Spirit has been active in the church since Pentecost, teaching and guiding according to Christ's promise, we should expect to find that at many points all Christian traditions mirror truth truly, even though at other points they appear flawed. Traditions are unlikely to be either wholly right or wholly wrong, but in the light of the Spirit's covenanted ministry we should expect them on the whole to be more right than wrong—and when we test them across the board by the Bible which they all seek to expound, this is what we find.

Imagine a millionaire exploring a great department store, saying of every item on display which he or she likes, "I'll have that," and so piling up a vast stock of delightful purchases. That is a picture of each Christian's privilege in relation to the varied traditions of the different segments of Christ's one church.

A well-known American reviewer (name withheld) once commended John Stott for not writing in a way that shows him to be an Anglican, as that man J. I. Packer regrettably does. Well, I am indeed an Anglican, and there is an eclectic quality in Anglicanism that may have helped me to see the point I am now making—but the privilege of claiming as one's own anything in any Christian tradition that appears good and wise is a privilege that belongs to every Christian, not just to Anglicans. To enrich our own Christianity by ransacking the traditional wealth of all Christendom is open to each of us, if God gives us sense enough to do it. I for one have been vastly enriched by writers and preachers, past and present, who were not Anglicans—more so, perhaps, than by those who were. I admit to thinking that Anglican heritage is the most nourishing in the Christian world, but what I owe to the Puritan tradition from John Owen to Charles Spurgeon and to the Welsh Nonconformist tradition in some of its latter-day representatives is more than I can measure. Both of these traditions seem to (doubtless blinkered) me to have had blind spots of their own, but they have been vastly profitable to me nonetheless. I should like to think that other Christians were seeking and finding similar enlargement of understanding from traditions not their own.

To sum up: It will not be enough to fight and win the battle for biblical inspiration and infallibility if we are then going to lose the battle for understanding the Bible and learning to live under its authority. We must be clear therefore on the rules of biblical interpretation, and with that work constantly to get the blinders (blinkers) off our spiritual eyes so that breadth and depth of practical insight may be ours at all points. If we want God to give us understanding, this is the way we must go. I ask you now to judge what I have said, and if you agree with it to do something about it.

5

MOUTHPIECE FOR GOD
Preaching and the Bible

At the time of the Reformation, when vernacular Bibles were appearing all over Europe and literacy was being established in Western culture, it was insisted that the Bible is for reading and every Christian should get to know it from cover to cover. This was right, as it still is. Holy Scripture is, as we have seen, the source and channel for our knowledge of God and his salvation. It is from Bible stories and Bible teachings, Bible promises and Bible warnings, biblical examples of godliness and its opposite, biblical reflections on wisdom and folly, and supremely from the biblical portrayal of the person, words, works, place and grace of our Lord Jesus Christ, that we learn the way of eternal life. Moreover, Bible knowledge has always been basic to Christian culture. Bible stories and standards were passed on by word of mouth in the darkest and most illiterate of the Dark and Middle Ages, and for four centuries more after the Reformers added to this heritage a clear understanding of the gospel. Thus it could truly be said that the Bible was the basis on which Western civilization was built. Fifty years of drift from these moorings since the second World War has left the West immeasurably poorer in spiritual capital, and the impoverishing continues. That the need for Christians to be soaked in Scripture is now greater than ever is a judgment with which most church-related people, of whatever denominational stripe, would heartily agree.

Not so, however, with the even stronger Reformation insistence that the Bible is for preaching, and that every minister should be first and foremost a constant, competent Bible expositor. The Reformers urged that the preaching of the Word is by God's appointment the prime means of grace to the church. The common objections to preaching nowadays are, first, that monologue is not the most efficient form of instruction and, second, that preachers' ideas, no matter how sincerely held and firmly stated, cannot carry God's authority. The first objection assumes that the purpose of preaching is to pass on information, as one would do in a lecture; the second assumes that there is no specific message from God for the preacher to deliver, so that all the preacher can ever do is relay his own best thoughts. I challenge both assumptions, the latter for reasons that this book has already made clear, and the former because the proper aim of preaching is to mediate meetings with God.

Anyone acquainted with the preaching career and sermonic legacy of such as (for instance) John Chrysostom, Augustine, Martin Luther, Hugh Latimer, John Knox, Richard Baxter, John Bunyan, George Whitefield, John Wesley,

Jonathan Edwards, Charles Simeon, Robert Murray McCheyne, Charles Spurgeon, John Charles Ryle, Martyn Lloyd-Jones, and Billy Graham, knows, first, that their goal in preaching was to become the means of God's encounter with their hearers, and second, that it was by focusing God's teaching in Scripture that they sought to achieve this purpose. Preaching, to them, was not so much searching out new truth (however new the truth they told might be to some listeners) as making vivid old truth in its relevance for living. Preaching, to them, was God-taught information set forth with God-given freedom and forthrightness in a God-prompted application; and they were sure that, as in apostolic days, so in their own and every subsequent era, preaching the Bible in this way was, remained, and ever would be basic for the health of the church. That is my belief, too, and my task in this chapter is to give it substance and teeth.

I shall, therefore, discuss in order the preparation, delivery, and hearing of sermons, viewing them as what ideally they are—human communications through which God himself communicates. I shall address throughout those who listen to sermons rather than those who preach them, and what I say about the preacher's disciplines of preparation and delivery will be said primarily to tune listeners in to their own discipline of receiving what is presented. Rather than risk generalizations about preaching that might seem to censure others whose style differs from mine, I have chosen to risk particularizations that may make me appear egotistic: that is, I shall lay myself on the line and explain in first-person terms how I seek to fulfill the preacher's role. Perhaps I should apologize for doing this, for I do not claim to be a major preacher. C. S. Lewis tells how he asked leave to write *The Problem of Pain* anonymously, since he would have to "make statements of such apparent fortitude that they would become ridiculous if anyone knew who made them." Anonymity was rejected, but he was informed that "I could write a preface explaining that I did not live up to my own principles! This exhilarating programme," Lewis continued, "I am now carrying out."[1] And I am doing something similar with regard to my preaching, sustained by the belief that you can sometimes do a useful job as a coach even when you are not one of the best players. But I venture upon this bit of ministerial strip-tease mainly because it will enable me to establish a frame of reference within which it will become very clear how sermons should be listened to and learned from.

Defining the Sermon

Within the established patterns of Christian worship, the Bible and its gospel get cast into bite-size discourses, usually between fifteen and fifty minutes long, with about half an hour as the median length. (A book of these discourses many years ago was titled *Thirty Minutes to Raise the Dead.*) We call them sermons, from the Latin *sermo*, which means a speech or spoken utterance. What sort of speech, now, is a sermon? Here is my definition; not all will endorse it: a theological liberal couldn't, and my guess is that many evangelicals, who could, don't and won't. (If my guess is wrong, no one will be happier than I am—nor, I think, more surprised!) I will state the definition, however, as plainly as I can, and my readers shall judge for themselves what acceptance it merits.

First, let me focus my definition. Sermons can be looked at from various angles and defined in a number of ways. An institutional definition of a sermon would describe it as a hortatory monologue delivered from a pulpit to people in pews as part of a liturgical program. A sociological definition would highlight the expectations that sermons seek to fulfill and the responsibilities that they are thought to impose. A homiletical definition would view the sermon as didactic communication, put over by means of a special rhetorical technique. Such definitions certainly have their place, but at this moment I am on a different track. The definition I offer—the definition with which I live, which commands my conscience and guides me in preparing specific messages—is theological (that is, trinitarian and theocentric) and functional (that is, centering on intention and effect).

This definition, or concept, was given me in embryo during the winter of 1948–49, when I was privileged on Sunday evenings to sit under the preaching of the late D. Martyn Lloyd-Jones at Westminster Chapel in London, England. Yehudi Menuhin has written of how overwhelmed he was the first time he played Beethoven's Violin Concerto under Wilhelm Furtwaengler, by reason of the power with which the great conductor recreated Beethoven's music all around him. Well, that was how I felt that winter as I heard Dr. Lloyd-Jones preach the gospel of Christ from the Gospel of Matthew, opening up Matthew 11 with magisterial weight and passion in some twenty discourses.[2]

Since then I have lived, worshiped, and preached under an ineffaceable sense of the authority of what Dr. Lloyd-Jones was doing. It is only in recent years, however, that I have been able to verbalize it to myself and others in a way that seems to me anything like adequate to the reality. And even so, my definition may not communicate all that from my standpoint it expresses, for preaching is ordinarily caught by contact rather than taught by rote. If my readers, preachers though they themselves may be, have never experienced such preaching as I encountered nearly fifty years ago, they may well miss much of the meaning of my words. Nonetheless, I hope that my definition will in fact strike some sparks.

A sermon, then, is *an applicatory declaration, spoken in God's name and for his praise, in which some part of the written Word of God delivers through the preacher some part of its message about God and godliness in relation to those whom the preacher addresses.* This definition, so far as I am concerned, is universally applicable. All sermons are topical in the sense of being about something specific, which can be indicated in a title. But no discourse is a *sermon* unless it is textual in the sense of being a Bible passage, text, or phrase delivering through the speaker some part of its own message as a word from God. Discourses that are not expository in this sense (I am talking about substance, not style or format) are simply not sermons: *addresses* may be a proper label for them, but *sermons* is a misnomer.

From this you can see that my definition grounds a particular view of the preacher's task on a particular view of the nature of Scripture. Fuller explanation is needed on both these matters, and it is convenient to take them in reverse.

The Nature of Scripture

Holy Scripture, the inspired Word (message) of the living

God, may truly be described as God preaching—preaching, that is, in the sense of instructing, rebuking, correcting, and directing every reader and hearer for the furthering of faith, praise, holiness, and spiritual growth. God preaches thus in and through all the various stories, sermons, soliloquies, schedules, statistics, songs, and supplications that make up the individual books of the canon. All that Bible writers tell us about God and humanity, God himself tells us; for the sacred text is not just human witness to God, but is also, and indeed primarily, God's own witness to himself, given us in this human form. Everything in Scripture teaches something of the Father's plan, something of the ministry and majesty of the Son as fulfiller of it, and something, too, about the gift and glory of eternal life and the way to set forth God's praise. Furthermore, it teaches this as from God himself. The approach to Scripture followed by preachers in the older Reformational-Puritan-Pietist-Evangelical tradition, from Luther to Lloyd-Jones, was determined by the clarity with which they grasped this truth, and it is our own urgent need to get back on this wavelength. Only as God himself is perceived to be preaching in our sermons can they have genuine spiritual significance, and God will be perceived to speak through us preachers only as we are enabled to make plain the fact that it is really the Bible that is doing the talking.

The Task of the Preacher

Since the Triune God—the Father and the Son, through the Spirit—already preaches to us in every part of the Bible, the human preacher's task resolves into becoming a mouthpiece and sounding board for the divine message that meets him in the text. It is not for the preacher to stand, as it were, in front of and above the Bible, setting himself between it and the people and speaking for it, as if it could not speak for itself. Rather, his role is to stand behind and below it, letting it deliver its own message through him and putting himself explicitly and transparently under the authority of that message, so that his very style of relaying it models a response to it. From this standpoint preaching is, indeed, in Phillips Brooks's phrase, "truth through personality" and the preacher is, indeed, half of his sermon. Only as he manifests both the mentality of a messenger and the disposition of a disciple will the preacher communicate any sense of God speaking in what he says. Insofar as he fulfills these two roles, his preaching will be genuinely prophetic: he will speak from God in his character as a servant of God. The Holy Spirit who enables him to do this will lead God's people to recognize God's authority in what he is saying. The form of authority that is acknowledged in Scripture as authentically moral and spiritual is the authority of God himself speaking, not of his spokesmen save as they echo and embody his word. That is how it is here. The authentic authority of the pulpit is the authority, not of the preacher's eloquence, experience, or expertise, but of God speaking in Scripture through what he says as he explains and applies his text.

So the preacher, rather than the critical commentator or the academic theologian, is the true interpreter of Scripture; for the preacher is the person whose privilege it is to bridge the apparent gap between the Bible and the modern world by demonstrating the relevance of what Scripture says to the lives of those whom he addresses.

Interpretation, as such, means among other things, bringing literary and artistic legacies to life and showing their significance for those who stand at a distance, temporal or cultural or both, from the producers of these materials. Biblical interpretation is a particular example of this. It involves both grammatical-historical exposition of what the text meant as instruction for the writer's envisaged readership, and contemporary application of it at the level of principle to show what it means for us today and what response it (or, rather, God in it) is calling for. Commentaries and theologies are resources for this task, but only preachers can fully perform it; and they perform it fully only as they apply their text in a rational and realistic way. To pass on biblical content, unapplied, is only to teach, not to preach. A lecture, as such, is not a sermon. Preaching is teaching plus—plus what? Plus application of truth to life. One's adequacy as a preacher, interpreting God's Word to God's people, is finally determined not by the erudition of one's exegesis but by the depth and power of one's application. This is the next matter that my definition of a sermon requires me to discuss.

The Theory of Application

A largely forgotten part of the evangelical heritage with regard to preaching is the procedure sometimes called "discriminating application," which Puritan writers were the first to formulate. I offer now a functional analysis of application, formally and schematically viewed, which is essentially a restatement in modern terms of what this procedure requires. Three guidelines are involved.

First, application should constantly focus on the unchanging realities of each person's relationship to God. The most important question that anybody ever faces is the issue of one's relationship with God. Both exposition and application in preaching must center here. Within the Bible story, cultures and circumstances changed and the externals of worship and devotion took different forms at different times. The New Testament era saw the coming of God incarnate, the establishing of Christ's kingdom, the eschatological gift of the Spirit, the superseding of ethnic Jewishness by a global outlook, and the new reality of life in Christ. But the basic elements in relating rightly to our holy, gracious Creator remained in essence the same from Genesis to Revelation, and are so still. These elements include faith, love, hope, obedience; humility, repentance, forgiveness, fidelity; thankful praise and trustful prayer; stewarding gifts, sanctifying one's activities, serving others, and standing against evil both in one's own heart and in the world outside. These are the unchanging realities that the preacher's elucidations of Scripture, whatever else they deal with, must regularly highlight and illustrate, and that his applications, one way or another, must regularly cover. The Bible is given us to teach us godliness. All our preaching ought to further that purpose.

Second, application should constantly focus on the person, place, and power of Jesus Christ. The Bible in its entirety is witness to Christ and to the Father's plans involving him. By setting these before us it makes us "wise for salvation" through faith in him (2 Tim. 3:15). Central to application in preaching, therefore, is the task of systematically relating God's love in Christ to the whole range of needs and perplexities to which, as we say (with truth), "Christ is the answer." This requires us both to dwell on his mediatorial office as our prophet, priest, and king, and also to present his person as set forth in the Gospels, so that he will be known and trusted as the individual that he was and is and will never be reduced to an unknown x in theological equations.

Yet, just as it would not be enough to require faith in the office and work of Christ without delineating his personal profile in this way, so too it is not enough to exhibit Jesus the man as our example and ignore the work of his saving lordship—which is a continuing defect, unhappily, of the Protestant liberal tradition. In application, the compassionate wisdom of the man from Galilee dealing with various kinds of sinners must be brought to bear together with the saving power of

> Jesus! my Shepherd, Husband, Friend,
> My Prophet, Priest, and King,
> My Lord, my Life, my Way, my End.

Only so will application be fully Christian, and fully effective.

Third, application should constantly search the hearts and consciences of the hearers. It is the preacher's responsibility to plan the applicatory part of the sermon to this end, so that the message is "homecoming" (Alexander Whyte's word) in a specific way to as many of his congregation as possible. In every congregation there are likely to be people in each of the following categories (which, as will be seen, are not entirely exclusive):

1. Unconverted and self-satisfied, needing to be awakened and humbled;
2. Concerned and inquiring, wanting to be told what being a Christian today involves;
3. Convicted and seeking, needing to be guided directly to Christ;
4. Young Christians who need to be built up and led on;
5. Mature Christians, aging both physically and spiritually, who need to be constantly encouraged, lest they flag;
6. People in trouble, through moral lapses, circumstantial traumas, "losses and crosses" (a Puritan phrase), disappointment, depression, and other such afflictions. It has been wisely observed that in every congregation there will be at least one broken heart.

Just as homemakers who prepare meals try to ensure that there will be enough kinds of food to satisfy all who are there, so too we who prepare sermons must try to see that, over a period of time if not in each single message, applications are made that will be home-coming and health-giving, through God's blessing, to each of these classes of people.

There are basically four types of application, each of which can be developed from any Bible truth about God and mankind, and each of which may and should be made from time to time to all six sorts of people. (Not that all twenty-four specific applications could actually be developed in one sermon! My point is that they are there to be developed, as wisdom directs.) There is, first, *application to our mind*, where the logical form is this: the truth presented shows us that we ought not to think thus-and-so (and if we have thought it up to now, we must stop thinking it);

instead, we should think such-and-such. Second, there is *application to our will,* where the logical form is that the truth presented shows us we ought not to behave thus-and-so (and if we have started, we must stop at once); instead, we ought to do such-and-such. Third, there is *application to our motivating drives,* where the logical form is this: the truth presented shows us that if we are living as we should and want to, we have very good reason and every encouragement to carry on, and if we are not living so, we have very good reason and every encouragement to change our ways. Fourth, there is *application to our condition,* where the logical form is found in the question: How do we stand in relation to the truth presented? Have we faced it, taken it to heart, measured and judged ourselves by it? How do we stand in relation to the God who speaks it to us? It is through these four types of application, whether made to us from the pulpit or by us to ourselves in private meditation, that Scripture fulfills to us its appointed function of correcting, rebuking, and training in righteousness (2 Tim. 3:16).

How the preacher will express and angle each type of application on each occasion is something that he must of necessity decide in light of what truth he is applying, what he knows about those he is addressing, what was said to them by himself or by others in previous sermons, and a host of other factors. A good rule of thumb for pastoral sermons, however, is that half the message should be in essence instruction in biblical truth about God and man and half should be in essence specific application of that truth. Observing these proportions, it seems to me, one cannot go far wrong.

Preparing the Sermon

How do I prepare my own sermons? The short answer is that I try to produce messages that conform to the specifications already set out. Being an academic without a stated pastoral charge, I often find myself preaching to congregations about which I know very little, but I sieve my material as best I can through my applicatory grid in hope of ensuring that I shall say something relevant and timely to as many as possible of the six types of people who I expect will be there.

Where do sermon messages come from? For most preachers, I think, and certainly for me, there are two main sources: first, the known needs of congregations, which suggest particular themes and passages on which to preach, and maybe even series of sermons; second, our own experience of being taught and disciplined by God, which leaves us with insights and wisdom that we find ourselves wanting to pass on. Sometimes a lectionary or prior church decision prescribes on which passage one must preach. In that case, one will search it and meditate and pray over it, seeking in it an important truth with an application that one has the skill to handle. Sometimes the occasion (Christmas, Easter, Pentecost, a national crisis, or some other event) dictates one's theme; then one will seek a passage to expound and apply appropriately. I would add here that a rounded theological understanding of the will and ways of God, and of the nature, demands, and resources of the Christian life is a great help in enabling one to see what truth one is looking at in particular Bible passages. Calvin's *Institutes*, covering these themes in classical fashion, is one theological guide that has suggested to me many messages over the years, and the writings of the two greatest Puritans, John Owen and Richard Baxter, have done the same.

What routines and resources do I use in preparing sermons? My method (which I share because my strategy in this chapter requires it, without wishing to make rules for anyone else) is, so to speak, first to walk round my text, or whatever I suspect will be my text (for at first, I am not always sure about that), looking at it in its larger context (i.e., as part of the book from which it comes, and of the Bible as a whole), and scribbling possible schemes of points to teach, angles of interaction with life and its problems to pursue, and personal applications to develop. I find that I need to start this process several days before the message has to be produced, for getting an outline that seems right—that is, one that expresses my heart and that I see how to use in searching the hearts of others—often takes me quite some time.

The outline is crucially important. When we preach, our hearers need to feel that we know where we are going and what we are aiming at; that the text is talking, that the flow of thought is logical and natural, that each application comes directly from the exposition, and that there is no change of thematic horses in midstream. Sermons that lack these modes of rationality will also lack persuasive power and authority. So, my outline needs to be thought through both forwards and backwards: forwards, from the opening sentence to each point of application, to make sure that the logical line is straight; backwards, from the envisaged applications to the exposition of the truths being applied, to make sure they are aptly and sufficiently stated for my applicatory purpose. Getting a workable outline that passes these tests is usually, I find, the hardest part of sermon preparation.

Only when I think I see my way to a compelling outline do I turn to the church's expository legacy of commentaries and homiletical materials, exploring it and drawing on these to fill out the scheme I already have. I find that reading others' work before my own outline is clear makes it harder, rather than easier, to settle in my mind what my message from the text is supposed to be. Biblical texts differ: some are directly didactic, others indirectly so; some state, some narrate, some illustrate; some are already applicatory in their form and thrust; some are exemplary, showing the root or fruit of godly or ungodly behavior. But all have living before the face of God as their reference point, and the most helpful resources at this stage are those that are most God-centered. For the record (though I do not suppose I am typical in this), modern expositions do not help me half as much as does Matthew Henry, the Puritan; and modern printed sermons do not suggest to me half as much as do those of C. H. Spurgeon and the sermonic writings of J. C. Ryle. As for illustrations, whenever I can, I use Bible stories to illustrate Bible doctrine. Beyond this, I find that there are usually illustrations enough in everyday events. For me, at least, exotic illustrations turn preaching into a performance remote from life, so that sermon time ceases to be an encounter with God and becomes an entertainment break, and accordingly, I expend no effort in hunting for them.

How much preparatory writing do I do? As much as is necessary to ensure that I know my message and have

words at my command to make all my points, both expository and applicatory, in a clear, pointed, weighty way that
gives no offense other than the inescapable offense of the
gospel itself. How much writing is needed to get to this
point varies, I find, from preacher to preacher.

How much written material do I take with me to the
pulpit? As much as I need to be exact, as well as free and
spontaneous, in the way that I speak. This, for me, means a
half sheet of paper, with skeletal notes in abbreviations of
my own devising, for each half-hour of talk. Some preachers need less, some more. Some need to have a complete
script with them, not to read word for word, but to give
them confidence as they speak, knowing that should words
suddenly fail to come spontaneously they can drop their
eyes to the script and find there what they need to start the
flow again.

Furtwaengler, whom I mentioned earlier, was always
thorough in his orchestral rehearsals, describing them as
his preparation for improvising at the performance. In the
same way thorough preparation equips the preacher to be
spontaneous in the pulpit. Fumbling spontaneity, which
indicates insufficient preparation, is always a depressant,
but controlled creativity, carrying the sense that the person
knows what he is doing even though he is doing some of it
on the spur of the moment, generates a sort of communica-
tive electricity that keeps people on the edge of their seats.
So it was when Furtwaengler played Beethoven, Brahms,
and Brückner. So it was when Dr. Lloyd-Jones preached, as
I can testify. So I pray, over and over, that it will be each
time I preach. I hope that any preachers who read this do
the same.

The Act of Preaching

Two generations ago, W. H. Griffith Thomas offered young preachers the following formula:

> Think yourself empty; read yourself full; write yourself clear; pray yourself keen; then into the pulpit, and let yourself go![3]

His sprightly words should not be understood as sanctioning the frivolity of exhibitionist exuberance, but simply as pinpointing the course that the serious preacher will follow. That preaching is indeed serious business should be clear by now; the glory of God and the issues of eternity are so directly bound up with the preaching of the Word that a casual or offhand attitude by its practitioners would be scandalous. But a serious approach to the preacher's work is spiritually demanding. Said Charles Simeon nearly two centuries ago:

> It is easy for a minister to prate in the pulpit, and even to speak much good matter; but to preach is not easy—to carry his congregation on his shoulders as it were to heaven; to weep over them, pray for them, deliver the truth with a weeping, praying heart; and if a minister has grace to do so now and then, he ought to be very thankful.[4]

To take one's preaching seriously is nervously demanding, too, if my experience is any guide: I lecture on a regular basis as well as preach, and find preaching to be far and away the more draining of the two activities. And no wonder!—for whereas one lectures to clear heads and ripen minds, one preaches to change lives and save souls. No doubt there are frivolous and irresponsible pulpiteers who do not feel the weight of their work, but I write at this moment as one of those who do, and so I now raise in blunt form the question: Given verbal efficiency in saying what you mean (we have already dealt with that), what further demands does the delivering of sermons make on the preacher? We have looked at the discipline of preparing them; what more, now, is involved in the further discipline of actually preaching them?

An answer of classic depth and strength was given to this question by Richard Baxter in *The Reformed Pastor*, dated 1656.

Be . . . careful that your graces are kept in vigorous and lively exercise, and that you preach to yourselves the sermons which you study, before you preach them to others. . . . When your minds are in a holy, heavenly frame, your people are likely to partake of the fruits of it. . . . They will likely feel when you have been much with God: that which is most on your hearts, is likely to be most in their ears. I confess I must speak it by lamentable experience, that I publish to my flock the distempers of my own soul. When I let my heart grow cold, my preaching is cold; and when it is confused, my preaching is confused; and so I can oft observe also in the best of my hearers, that when I have grown cold in preaching, they have grown cold too; and the next prayers which I have heard from them have been too like my preaching. We are the nurses of Christ's little ones. If we forbear taking food ourselves, we shall famish them; it will soon be visible in their leanness. . . . If we let our love decline, we are not likely to raise up theirs. . . . Whereas, if we abound in faith, and love, and zeal, how would it overflow to the refreshing of our congregations, and how would it appear in the increase of the same graces in them! O brethren, watch therefore over your own hearts: keep out lusts and passions, and worldly inclinations; keep up the life of faith, and love, and zeal; be much at home, and much with God. If it be not your daily business to study your own hearts, and to subdue corruption, and to walk with God—if you make not this a work to which you constantly attend, all will go wrong, and you will starve your hearers; or, if you have an affected fervency, you cannot expect a blessing to attend it from on high. Above all, be much in secret prayer and meditation. Thence you must fetch the heavenly fire that must kindle your sacrifices: remember, you cannot decline and neglect your duty to your own hurt alone; many will be losers by it as well as you. For your people's sake, therefore, look to your hearts. . . .

A minister should take some special pains with his heart, before he is to go to the congregation: if it be then cold, how is he likely to warm the hearts of his hearers? Therefore, go then specially to God for life: read some rousing, awakening book, or meditate on the weight of the subject of which you are to speak, and on the great necessity of your people's souls, that you may go in the zeal of the Lord into his house.[5]

Powerful stuff, you will agree, and as challenging today as

it was when first written. What Baxter calls for is not pulpit dramatics or simulated passion (that is what he means by "affected fervency"); it is, rather, consecrated concentration on the task of persuading the congregation to receive and respond to the truth from God that one is presenting. The preacher must be clear that he is in the pulpit not to give his own opinions on things, but to relay a God-given message and to do so in a way that shows that he himself is as much under its authority as anyone. So his goal must be to speak from his heart in a way that expresses his sincerity, his faithfulness to God's Word, and his seriousness about the glory of God and the good of souls; and to do this in the way that is natural to him, and therefore makes him transparent to his hearers. Baxter was a man of passionate intellect and torrential rhetoric; another preacher will be slower-moving and more low-key in style, more or less didactic, humorous, analytical, and anecdotal, according to how God made him. The point is not that all preachers should speak in the same way, but that every preacher should speak in a way that makes plain, first that his message is from God who speaks it in Scripture, second that he himself comes from the presence of God to deliver it, and third that it matters to him that his hearers follow the path of life by receiving it rather than miss that path by rejecting it. This is my aim when I preach, and if what has been said up to this point is right, it is surely clear that it ought to be every other preacher's aim too. It is for the achieving of this aim, rather than for any sort of personal experience as such, that the anointing of the Holy Spirit upon us should be sought when we are to preach, and in terms of the achieving of this aim that God's anointing should actually be defined.[6]

How to Hear Sermons

"We also thank God continually," wrote Paul, "because, when you received the word of God, which you heard from us, you accepted it not as the word of men, but as it actually is, the word of God, which is at work in you who believe" (1 Thess. 2:13). If true Christian preaching is as described in the foregoing pages, then it too, like Paul's preaching, is the Word of God for substance, as indeed the Reformers insisted it was, and the question for us is thus: how are we to hear sermons as the Word of God and benefit from them in our ongoing relationship with God? In his *Christian Directory* (1673) Richard Baxter addresses this question in a way that is worth quoting at some length.

> **Directions for . . . Understanding the Word which you Hear.**
>
> I. Read and meditate on the holy Scriptures much in private, and then you will be the better able to understand what is preached on it in public, and to try that doctrine, whether it be of God. . . .
>
> II. Live under the clearest, [most] distinct, convincing teaching that you possibly can procure. . . . Ignorant teachers . . . are unlike[ly] to make you men of understanding; as erroneous teachers are unlike[ly] to make you orthodox and sound.
>
> III. Come not to hear with a careless heart, . . . but

come with a sense of the unspeakable weight, necessity, and consequence of the holy word which you are to hear: and when you understand how much you are concerned in it, and truly love it, as the word of life, it will greatly help your understanding of every particular truth. . . .

IV. Suffer not vain thoughts or drowsy negligence to hinder your attention. . . be as earnest and diligent in attending and learning, as you would have the preacher be in teaching. . . .

VIII. Meditate on what you hear when you come home. . . .

VI. Inquire, where you doubt, of those that can resolve and teach you. It showeth a careless mind, and a contempt of the word of God, in most people . . . that never come to ask the resolution of one doubt . . . though they have pastors . . . that have ability, and leisure, and willingness to help them.

Directions for Remembering what you Hear.

I. It greatly helpeth memory to have a full understanding of the matter spoken which you would remember. . . . Therefore labour most for a clear understanding according to the last directions. . . .

III. Method is a very great help to memory. . . . Ministers must not only be methodical . . . but . . .

choose that method which is most easy to the hearers to understand and remember. . . .

IV. Numbers are a great help to memory. . . .

V. Names also and signal words are a great help to memory. . . . Therefore preachers should contrive the force of every reason, use, direction, [etc.] as much as may be, into some one emphatical word. (And some do very profitably contrive each of these words to begin with the same letter, which is good for memory. . . .) As if I were to direct you to the chiefest helps to your salvation, and should name, 1. Powerful preaching. 2. Prayer. 3. Prudence. 4. Piety. 5. Painfulness. 6. Patience. 7. Perseverance . . . the very names would help the hearers' memory. . . .

VII. Grasp not at more than you are able to hold, lest thereby you lose all. If there be more particulars than you can possibly remember, lay hold on some which most concern you, and let go the rest. . . .

VIII. Writing is an easy help for memory. . . .

IX. Peruse what you remember, or write it down, when you come home; and fix it speedily before it is lost. . . . Pray over it, and confer on it with others.

X. If you forget the very words, yet remember the main drift. . . . And then you have not lost the sermon, though you have lost the words; as he hath not lost his food, that hath digested it, and turned it into flesh and blood.

Directions for Holy Resolutions and Affections in Hearing. . . .

II. Remember that ministers are the messengers of Christ, and come to you on his business and in his name. . . .

III. Remember that God is instructing you, and warning you, and treating with you, about no less than the saving of your souls. . . .

VI. Make it your work with diligence to apply the word as you are hearing it. . . . You have work to do as well as the preacher, and should all the while be as busy as he: as helpless as the infant is, he must suck when the mother offereth him the breast; if you must be fed, yet you must open your mouths, and digest it, for another cannot digest it for you. . . . Therefore be all the while at work, and abhor an idle heart in hearing, as well as an idle minister.

VII. Chew the cud, and call up all when you come home in secret, and by meditation preach it over to yourselves. . . .

IX. Go to Christ by faith, for the quickening of his Spirit. . . . Entreat him to . . . open your hearts, and speak to you by his Spirit, that you may be taught of

God, and your hearts may be his epistles, and the tables where the everlasting law is written. . . .

Directions to bring what we Hear into Practice.

I. Be acquainted with the failings of your hearts and lives, and come on purpose to get directions and helps against those particular failings . . . say when you go out of doors, I go to Christ for physic for my own disease. . . .

IV. When you come home, let conscience in secret . . . repeat the sermon to you. Between God and your-selves, consider what there was delivered to you in the Lord's message, that your souls were most con-cerned in.

V. Hear the most practical preachers you can well get . . . that are still [constantly] urging you to holi-ness of heart and life, and driving home every truth to practice. . . .

VII. Associate yourselves with the most holy, seri-ous, practical Christians. . . .

VIII. Keep a just account of your practice; examine yourselves in the end of every day and week. . . . Call yourselves to account every hour, what you are doing and how you do it . . . and your hearts must be watched and followed like unfaithful servants, and like loitering scholars [schoolchildren], and driven on to every duty, like a dull or tired horse.

IX. Above all set your hearts to the deepest contemplations of the wonderful love of God in Christ, and the sweetness and excellency of a holy life, and the . . . glory which it tendeth to, that your souls may be in love with your dear Redeemer, and all that is holy, and love and obedience may be as natural to you. And then the practice of holy doctrine will be easy to you, when it is your delight.[7]

It seems to me that Baxter covers the entire waterfront here, and I do not see how a single sentence that I have quoted from him can be challenged by anyone who knows that the Bible is the word of God.

But the contrast between the hard-working, hard-thinking, purposeful way in which Baxter tells us to listen to the Word preached and the aimless, detached, passive frame of mind in which most of us today do listen to sermons could hardly be greater. Baxter's discipline of expecting, focusing, memorizing (writing notes if need be), discussing, praying, and applying is at the opposite extreme from our modern habit of relaxing at sermon-time, settling back in our seats to see if the preacher's performance will interest and entertain us, and if anything he says will particularly strike us—and if not, then to forget the sermon and to say if asked that we got nothing out of it. But even if the preacher is not operating in full accord with the principles that the present chapter lays down, this casual, unexpectant, prayerless, half-bored way of listening to his messages cannot be right. I remember one or two very elderly Christians in my youth who listened to sermons essentially in Baxter's way, expecting them to yield fodder for a week's meditation and soul-nourishment, including applicatory reflections going beyond what the preacher actually said. But this devotional style seems nowadays to have completely died out, so that it needs to be learned all over again, starting very much from scratch. The combined efforts of homiletics professors in seminaries training tomorrow's clergy, senior ministers guiding junior members of their team, and preaching pastors leveling with their congregations about what it means for them to preach and for people to hear the Word of God, would seem to be needed to get the church back on track at this point. A great deal of work will have to be done if sermons are to be restored to their proper place as a means of grace in our Christian lives.

What should you and I be doing meanwhile? We should start taking seriously the sermons that we actually hear. We should pray beforehand for the preacher and for ourselves, that God will prepare us for each other in such a way that through the sermon he may draw near to meet us himself. We should labor to be alert, expectant, and attentive as the sermon is preached, making notes if need be to ensure that we remember what we are hearing, and asking ourselves all the time what the message is showing us of God's glory, of our own needs and shortcomings, and of God's help for us in and through Christ. We should discuss the sermon afterwards with other Christians to make sure we saw the full point of it. We should meditate on it, pray that God will bless to us the truth we found in it, and start acting on any words of correction or direction in it that we know apply to us. A month of this, and if the preaching we have heard is thin gruel by biblical standards, we shall have earned the right to ask our preachers to thicken the biblical substance of their messages so that we shall not any more have to go hungry through the week. This is a contribution to the upgrading of preaching that any lay person can make, and it will be a happy thing when layfolk begin to make it.

When should we start this routine of serious listening? Why, next Lord's Day, of course. When else?

6

LIFE AND HEALTH AND PEACE
Christians and Their Bibles

The title of this chapter brings together three of the weightiest and richest words that Scripture uses for the renewed existence of those who know God's sovereign grace. Each of these words has an everyday meaning—life and health referring to one's physical condition, and peace signifying inner and outer calm—but here what they express is the spiritual well-being of the born-again. *Life*— eternal life, as the New Testament regularly calls it—is the state in which one recognizes, receives, and responsively relates to God in Jesus Christ: in other words, Jesus Christ the Lord in his identity as God the Redeemer, who now calls us into fellowship with himself and with God the Father through God the Holy Spirit. *Health* is a concept focused by the New Testament adjective *healthy,* which has traditionally been translated "sound" (as when we describe horses as sound in wind and limb); it is the state of well-being in which our spiritual system functions steadily and strongly the way it should, in faith, hope, and love Godward. *Peace* is a word of wide meaning that covers the state of being divinely pardoned and accepted; of knowing that this acceptance, based on Christ's cross, is solid and lasting fact; of accepting and loving oneself as the person God made in his image and loves and has redeemed and is restoring; of accepting one's circumstances, whatever they are, as divinely ordered for one's good; of facing the unknown future in calm reliance on God's promises; and of refusing to respond in kind to any violence and hostility shown to one by others. Life, health, and peace are three words that between them sum up the essence of Christian life.

The point becomes more vivid by contrast. The reality of *life* is opposed to the state of unresponsiveness to God, which is called death in Ephesians 2:1, 5, and Colossians 2:13 on the analogy of a corpse, which is totally unresponsive to any stimulus of any kind. The reality of *health* is opposed to the inner sickness of unloving, self-serving, God-defying lifestyles, which exhibit human nature out of sorts and indeed wasting away; for these are the degenerative diseases of the soul. The reality of *peace* is opposed to the stress and strain, the anxious, fearful, troubled, resentful, bitter, vengeful, addictive, adversarial way of living that so many moderns and postmoderns are anchored in nowadays. By contrast with these wretched alternatives, life, health, and peace appear as words of deliverance and delight.

The first to link these precious words together was Charles Wesley, in a classic celebration of the impact of Jesus

Christ, known and understood for what he is, on benighted humans:

> O for a thousand tongues to sing
> My great Redeemer's praise,
> The glories of my God and King,
> The triumphs of his grace!
>
> Jesus—the name that charms our fears,
> That bids our sorrows cease;
> 'Tis music in the sinner's ears;
> 'Tis life and health and peace.

But these words may with equal fitness be applied to the impact of the Holy Scripture upon us. Look at the following, by other Christian poets. First, Anne Steele:

> Father of mercies, in thy word
> What endless glory shines!
> For ever be thy name adored
> For these celestial lines.
>
> Here the Redeemer's welcome voice
> Spreads heavenly peace around;
> And life and everlasting joys
> Attend the blissful sound.
>
> Here springs of consolation rise
> To cheer the fainting mind:
> And thirsty souls receive supplies,
> And sweet refreshment find.

Now look at this by Henry Williams Baker:

Lord, thy word abideth,
And our footsteps guideth;
Who its truth believeth
Light and joy receiveth.

Who can tell the pleasure,
Who recount the treasure
By thy word imparted
To the simple-hearted?

Word of mercy, giving
Succour to the living;
Word of life, supplying
Comfort to the dying.

O that we discerning
Its most holy learning,
Lord, may love and fear thee,
Evermore be near thee.

And at this, by Bernard Barton:

Lamp of our feet, whereby we trace
Our path when wont to stray;
Stream from the fount of heavenly grace,
Brook by the traveller's way;

Bread of our souls, whereon we feed,
True manna from on high;

Our guide and chart, wherein we read
Of realms beyond the sky;

Word of the ever-living God,
Will of his glorious Son,
Without thee how could earth be trod,
Or heaven itself be won?

Lord, grant that we aright may learn
The wisdom it imparts,
And to its heavenly teaching turn
With simple, childlike hearts.

The thought that all these lyrics express is that the gift of
life and health and peace comes to us from God through
Holy Scripture.

Christ and the Bible

The link between Christ and the Bible, as previous chapters
have shown, is direct, organic, and multiple; so it is only
true to say that life and health and peace come from either
if at once you add that they come from the one through the
other—from Christ, that is, through the Scriptures, or from
the Scriptures through Christ. Various aspects of the connection have already passed before us. The canonical Scriptures of the two Testaments are the interpretative and
applicatory record of God's redemptive program in history,
the program that has now climaxed in the life, death, resurrection, enthronement, and present heavenly ministry of
the Lord Jesus and in the ongoing pentecostal ministry of

the Holy Spirit. These Scriptures are also, and equally, a revelation from God: a revelation of his own identity, character, and purposes; of his wisdom, will, and ways for achieving our salvation; of his words of specific instruction, partly indicative, partly imperative, for the sanctifying of our lives; and of his invitation to the world to turn to Christ and find life. The meaning of biblical inspiration is that through the agency of the sovereign Holy Spirit the sacred text is at once God's didactic witness and man's celebratory witness to salvation through Christ—eternally planned, long prepared for, accomplished through incarnation at the appointed time, and now to be proclaimed everywhere as Scripture sets it forth. The person and place of the Christ of space-time history is the interpretative key to all Scripture; the Old Testament is to be read in the light of its New Testament fulfillment in and by him, just as the New Testament is to be read in the light of its Old Testament foundations on which that fulfilment rested. For the Christian there is no Christ but the Christ of the Bible (specifically, of the New Testament teachers), and no understanding of the Bible but that which matches the expressed mind of Christ and his apostles (specifically, as they interpret the Old Testament and relate themselves to it).

As regards authority, it is impossible to give too much weight to the fact that Jesus, who was himself God speaking, should have consistently viewed the words of his Bible as God speaking, and should have lived his life and fulfilled his vocation of teaching and suffering in direct and conscious obedience to what was written. Now, in effect, from his throne he tells all who would be his disciples that they must learn from him and follow his example at this

point and submit to becoming disciples of the canonical
Scriptures. His authority and its for us are one. What then
should we do? We should look to the Holy Spirit, who
inspired the biblical text and who authenticates it to regen-
erate hearts as God-given by sensitizing us to the impact of
its divinity, to make clear to us not only what God said in
and through the text to its original readers, but also what
he says to us via the same text here and now. We should
ask for the Spirit's illumination, especially for our attempts
at applicatory thinking. We should settle it in our minds
that everything the Father and the Son say to us in and
through Scripture relates, one way or another, to the person, place, and purpose of Christ, to the realities of God's
kingdom, and to faithful following of Christ through what
Bunyan called the wilderness of this world. That is what
the Christian Bible is all about, and we are not to go off at
tangents away from this when we read it. We are always to
remember that whatever the Bible teaches has divine
authority, and we are to bow to that authority at every
point, confessing that here we have both truth and wisdom. This is the way of true discipleship, the path of life
and health and peace.

The Holy Spirit and the Bible

Earlier we heard Charles Wesley telling us that the source
of life and health and peace is the name, meaning the
knowledge, of the Lord Jesus Christ. It is fitting now to
quote him again as he invokes the Holy Spirit to mediate
through Scripture the communion with Christ out of which
our new existence comes. It is a recurring reality of Chris-

tian experience that those who explore the Bible with a
purpose of humble obedience to all the Spirit shows them
in the text find that the fruit of their exploring is more than
factual knowledge of God's work and will; it is in truth
fellowship with their Lord in person. Conviction of truth,
consecration of heart, communion with Christ, and confidence in his love, become aspects of a single ball of wax (I
express myself the American way) when Christians open
themselves to what the Westminster Confession I.x calls
"the Holy Spirit speaking in the Scripture." In John Wesley's *Collection of Hymns for the Use of the People called Methodists* (1779), these verses by Charles are set to be sung
"Before the Reading of the Scriptures":

> Come, Holy Ghost, (for mov'd by thee
> The prophets wrote and spoke:)
> Unlock the Truth, thyself the Key,
> Unseal the sacred Book.
> God, thro' himself, we then shall know,
> If thou within us shine:
> And sound, with all the saints below,
> The depths of love divine.

He also wrote this:

> Come, divine Interpreter,
> Bring us eyes thy Book to read,
> Ears the mystic words to hear,
> Words which did from thee proceed,
> Words that endless bliss impart,
> Kept in an obedient heart.

And this:

> When quiet in my house I sit,
>   Thy Book be my companion still,
> My joy thy sayings to repeat,
>   Talk o'er the records of thy will,
> And search the oracles divine
> Till every heartfelt word be mine.
>
> O may the gracious words divine
>   Subject of all my converse be!
> So will the Lord his follower join,
>   And walk and talk himself with me;
> So shall my heart his presence prove,
> And burn with everlasting love.

The approach to Scripture, the valuation of it, and the expectations from it, that Charles Wesley expresses here are
in no way unique or eccentric; rather, this is the charac-
teristically Christian perspective. Wesley is in the mainstream. So is his contemporary, William Cowper, who in his
days of Christian sanity, before the delusion of damnation
struck him, connected the divinity of the Scriptures, the
Spirit's help in exploring them, the reality of fellowship
with Christ through them, and the resulting state of love,
joy, and hope (to which, as is plain, life, health, and peace
correspond) in a similar fashion:

> The Spirit breathes upon the Word
>   And brings the truth to sight;

> Precepts and promises afford
>   A sanctifying light.
>
> A glory gilds the sacred page,
>   Majestic, like the sun:
> It gives a light to every age;
>   It gives, but borrows none.
>
> My soul rejoices to pursue
>   The steps of him I love,
> Till glory breaks upon my view
>   In brighter worlds above.

Such verses strike an echo in the heart of mainstream Christians everywhere.

Bible Moths

I wrote above of Christians who *explore* the Bible. This is the point at which to say that the word *explore* takes us further into the way we should relate to Scripture than the familiar words *read* and *study* do. Exploring is not, of course, less than reading and studying, but it is more. You can read books mechanically, without interest, and study facts mechanically, without focus, but exploring territory is a process of search, thought, and correlation that demands both interest and focus. Exploring Scripture is more than a routine for gathering data. It has to do with memorization, meditation, and interrogation. In exploring you poke, and dig, and ask questions, and make and test guesses, and try to see how everything ties in with everything else. Exploration is exciting! I spoke earlier of the need to ask what each biblical passage is saying about God and about the human condition and about one's own life. These are the questions with which biblical exploration begins, and it is through seeking the Holy Spirit's help in answering them that the knowledge of Jesus Christ, and of life and health and peace through him becomes ours.

The members of John Wesley's little society (we should call it, small group) at Oxford in the 1730s, the Holy Club as their detractors described them, were Bible explorers in this sense, and as a result they were ridiculed as "Bible moths," eating up scriptural teaching as moths eat woolen clothes. They were Bible moths before they came to saving faith in Christ, and they were right to be, and when they received full assurance they became more of Bible moths than they were before. I hope all who read this book can tell a comparable story.

But can we? Well-worn Bibles are rarities these days; in many homes there is no Bible at all, and the ignorance of what Scripture contains that has come to mark not only our secular community but our church attenders, too, is truly horrific. Not so long ago it was common for the Bible to be read at daily prayers in Western families and for children to be taught Bible stories at home, and it was a sign of an educated person to have some idea what the Bible is about, even if you made no Christian profession—but not anymore! And in too many churches the Bible has ceased to be an item of congregational use. For the preacher to speak with Bible in hand, turning up and citing Scripture as he goes along, is nowadays an unusual event, and as a direct consequence his hearers have no Bible in their hands either, even when one is set before them in the pew rack. They have learned that they are not likely to need a Bible in order to follow the sermon. The Sunday school will probably boast a range of visual aids for topical instruction, and the stories taught will be mostly from the Bible, but the Bible itself in the teacher's hand as authority and focus is missing more often, it seems, than not. The Bible remains the world's best seller, and no part of the human family has ever had so many accurate and attractive new translations to choose between as has the modern English-speaking West, nor so many dozens (yes, dozens!) of reliable study Bibles. Yet despite all this, it seems that on the whole the book of God is being less and less read. Bible moths today are few and far between.

But suppose one resolves before God to make the quest for life and health and peace through Jesus Christ one's priority, and to that end to become a latter-day Bible moth. How then should one view the Bible as one approaches it? To what wavelength of concentration and expectation should one's mind be tuned?

In academic biblical study, where the main concern, according to the conventions of the professional guild, is with the anatomy of past facts and the history of past ideas, the state of scholarly opinion is the springboard from which one starts, and biblical languages, biblical history, biblical criticism (investigating the origins and sources of the canonical books), the historical understanding of each book, sentence by sentence, in its socio-cultural context, and the varieties of biblical theology, are the main agenda items. For those whose vocational role is to preach and teach the Bible, these disciplines are of major importance, even though their bearing on relational knowledge of God here and now is only indirect. But I am posing the question of approach from the standpoint of seekers and saints as such—persons, that is, for whom relational knowledge of God and the receiving of life, health, and peace from Jesus Christ is what matters most. I shall now address this question directly, answering it in a way that is different from, and broader than (though not contrary to), the merely academic. Pulling together the threads of things that have been said in earlier chapters, I offer now a spectrum of seven points, each of which, I believe, highlights an aspect of the approach that is critical for the God-glorifying communion with Christ and enrichment from Christ that we all, I trust, are seeking.

One: A Library

First, think of the Bible as a *library*, a collection of 66 separate pieces of writing, some of them composite in themselves, one of them (the Psalter) consisting of 150 separate items. From the literary standpoint these books are a heterogeneous mix, histories and biographies rubbing shoulders with visions, sermons, poems, philosophical reflections, genealogies, statistics, rituals, and much else. But the books are bound together by a common purpose, and by an extraordinary unity of subject matter as they fulfill that common purpose. Their common purpose is to inform us about God and godliness, and to draw us, one way and another, into a responsive life of faith, hope, love, and praise. In light of the fact that these books were written over a period of something like 1,500 years in a number of different cultures, the unity of their presentation of God and his ways is simply stunning. In terms of basic principles about God's person, power, and plan, humankind's dignity and destiny, and the realities of God's saving grace, everything in the 66 books converges. Amazing? Yes, but demonstrably true. Grasp, then, the diversity of the Bible within its unity, and the unity of the Bible within its diversity.

Early in his career as a theologian, Karl Barth spoke of the "strange new world of the Bible"—the real, God-centered world that stands in stark contrast to the man-centered world that modern human beings, like their counterparts in Bible times, imagine instinctively, though improperly, that they occupy. In this strange new world, God the Creator appears as God the Redeemer, actively furthering a great plan for re-creating a race, and restoring a cosmos, that sin has spoiled. The backbone of the Bible is the narrative histories, from Genesis to Acts, telling of a covenant people, an exodus from captivity, a promised land, a monarchy that over the centuries became a focus of unfaithfulness, a national captivity and return from exile, a prophesied Savior who died and rose and reconstituted the covenant people in faith-union with himself, and an outpouring of the Holy Spirit to make the beginning of heaven's life a matter of experience here on earth. The rest of the biblical material is linked to this backbone in terms of its content, just as your rib cage, the other bits and pieces of your skeleton, and your nervous and muscular systems are linked one way or another to your backbone. The Old Testament prophetic books and wisdom books, and the New Testament epistles, explain and apply the truths about God that are displayed in the history and tell us how to live in response to them. The Psalter models for us the practice of prayer and praise, complaint and celebration, and the book of Revelation gives visions of final victory when Christ comes again. Such is the organism of Bible teaching; such is the vision of the world's story seen from God's point of view on which the sixty-six books converge.

This convergence is in fact a pointer to the nature of the books as revelation. Without in the least restraining or inhibiting the human factors in each compositional process, thereby diminishing the human quality of the work that resulted, God so guided and overruled the writing that the substance of what was written was his own true and trustworthy witness to himself, presented in the form of honest and well-meant witness to him by the human writers. Thus, as in prophecy and supremely in the incarnate life of the Son, God uses his gift to us of language to tell us things about himself. He is not the dumb God of philosophy since Kant, nor the feeble God of modern process theology, but the vocal Lord, sovereign in both speech and action. Words and deeds belong together in his self-disclosure. In his plan for world salvation through Christ he not only did what he intended, but both before and after the key events he spoke, using human language to tell his servants, and through them us, what was afoot and what had already been accomplished. Scripture might from this standpoint be labeled God's log book, his record of work decided on in advance and now definitively done. Such is the biblical revelation. The narratives, the explanations, the predictions, the mandatory and modeled responses, all come to us as direct verbal instruction from the God we serve. So the ideal way to introduce readings from Scripture in church (or anywhere else, for that matter) is with the venerable formula: "Hear the Word of God, as it is written in such-and-such a chapter of such-and-such a book." For when we hear Scripture read, or read it for ourselves, it is God's own utterance that we encounter, and we should never allow ourselves to think of it as anything less.

A common view in this century has been that though God is indeed the mighty Lord of history, he does not speak. What he does instead is illuminate the minds of good people so that they can guess more or less correctly the meaning of what he has been up to. So (it is argued) we should read Scripture as embodying a set of fairly shrewd guesses about God—guesses from which, however, we may allow ourselves to depart if we have sufficient reason, for after all no human guess has final authority. But this is wrong. The truer analogy is the requirement in Britain's advanced driving test that you give the examiner a running commentary on what you intend and foresee as you drive—why you are speeding up or slowing down, what hazards you detect and what action you are taking to meet them, and so on. God has acted like that: as he operated in history after the Fall to maintain justice, redeem sinners, and set up his kingdom, so he spoke to his people in prophecy and in narrative, in commentary and in commandment, to make plain to them what he was doing, why he was doing it, and what they and others should do about it; and in due course he prompted the recording of what he had said and shown so that it might be permanently and universally available. Holy Scripture is thus God's self-testimony, and its substantive content is, as Calvin puts it, *doctrina Dei*—teaching given, first to last, by God himself. The sixty-six books that make it up are all supernatural in this sense, that though their production involved something like forty human writers, the primary author of each single one of them is God. It is of crucial importance that we be clear on this.

Two: A Landscape

Second, see the Bible as a *landscape,* that is, a panorama of human life. Not only is it teaching from God about God, it is also a people-book, narrating stories of good and evil, faith and unbelief, obedience and disobedience, spiritual blessing and spiritual disaster, in the lives of some of the most vital, virile, forthright, fascinating people you can imagine. As we read their stories, we learn a steady flow of lessons about right and wrong ways to live; we are shown the moral and spiritual pitfalls that surround us and the triumphs in God that are possible for those who believe and do right; and we find ourselves encouraged, both outwardly and inwardly, to follow the good examples and avoid the bad ones. To explore the Bible from this point of view is absorbingly interesting and teaches many precious lessons for the managing of our own lives.

When people hear that the Bible is God's teaching, they often jump to the conclusion that the really significant parts of it must be the doctrinal generalizations (in Romans, Galatians, Ephesians, and Hebrews, for instance), and that the biographical material is unimportant by comparison. So, for instance, they may review the life of Abraham in Genesis with eyes only for its teaching on justification by faith and God's covenant of grace, plus its typical foreshadowing of Calvary at Mount Moriah, and they will miss altogether the lessons about faith and unbelief, fortitude and cowardice, patience and impatience, humility and boldness before God, spiritual immaturity and growth, and right and wrong ways of managing the marriage relationship, which are there for our learning in the story. The truth is that the Bible is jam packed with narrative material about godly and godless behavior, and it is full of wisdom about the business of living, most notably (you would expect this) in the Wisdom literature. Of the five Wisdom books of the Old Testament, it has been classically said (I think by Oswald Chambers though I cannot find the reference) that the Psalms will teach you how to pray, Proverbs how to live, Job how to suffer, the Song of Solomon how to love, and Ecclesiastes how to enjoy. That dictum seems to me wonderfully insightful: and it is totally reinforced by James, the New Testament Wisdom writer, who speaks to all these themes most forcefully within his five brief chapters.

So the landscape of life in Scripture, in both its biographical and its philosophical presentation, offers us lessons about practical godliness in abundance. Study Bible people and Bible wisdom, then, and you will learn much about serving and pleasing God.

Three: A Letter

Third, look upon the Bible as a *letter*, addressed to you personally by the divine Lord. To do this is not soft sentimentality, warm but fuzzy; it is hard theology, thoroughly thought through. Let me explain.

What is a letter? It is a written document addressed to a particular person or persons, expressing to them the writer's mind and thereby defining in some way the writer-reader relationship. There are business letters, love letters, circular letters, thank-you letters, begging letters, lawyer's letters, and many other kinds. The New Testament contains apostolic pastoral letters (Paul to the Thessalonians and the Corinthians, for example, whom he knew, and to the Romans, whom he did not know; John to the surviving community from which the Gnostic separatists had just walked out; and so on). These pastoral letters, sent out in love as a gesture of concern by a writer with authority, are the biblical items with which the Bible as a whole is most directly comparable. How so? In the fullness of his foreknowledge and the wisdom of his providence, God has so designed Holy Scripture that it comes to each of its readers on every occasion as a communication tailored to that reader's need, addressed to that reader's head and heart, and asking that reader for a specific response to what the divine writer is saying. For the breathtaking truth is that Holy Scripture in its entirety is the Word of God directed personally to everyone whom it reaches in order to set up, deepen, and enrich a personal love-relationship between the divine Sender and the human recipient.

You have a Bible, and in the front of it your name is written. Think of that as if the Lord himself had written it, as your human correspondents write your name on the envelopes in which they send you their letters. Think of your Bible as a gift received from the hand of the Lord Jesus, with the words: "Here is your handbook for following me." Think of each page as having the letters RSVP written at the head of it. A charming misprint on the contents page of a book I wrote long ago told the world that RSVP means Revised Standard Version, but of course it doesn't; RSVP is a request in French—*répondez s'il vous plaît,* reply if you please. That is what God, who gave us the Word and in whose presence we read, it says to us in effect all the time. The promised life and health and peace will not become ours without an appropriate response of thought, thanksgiving, trust, hope, praise, prayer, self-searching, repentance, or whatever to the things that we read.

It is not always noticed that the thought of the Bible as personal address is already present in the famous passage where Paul reminds Timothy of the source, function, and fruitfulness of Holy Scripture. Its presence, however, becomes evident if one follows the flow of thought. Paul is telling young Timothy that in the face of constant adverse pressures he must "continue in what you have learned and have become convinced of" (2 Tim. 3:14), and he gives him two reasons why. The first is "because you know those from whom you learned it"—his grandmother Eunice, his mother Lois, and Paul himself (1:5, 13), all of whom should have credibility in Timothy's eyes because of the power of faith he had seen in them. The second reason is that "from infancy you have known the Holy Scriptures, which are able to make you wise for salvation through faith in Christ Jesus" (3:15). The credibility of the Scriptures should be beyond doubt for Timothy, since "All Scripture is God-breathed" (3:16)—in other words, was produced by the Holy Spirit, who is God's creative breath. Says Psalm 33:6:

"By the word of the LORD were the heavens made, their starry host by the breath of his mouth"—a statement in the last words of which Christian readers rightly find a reference to the Holy Spirit, whose very name (*ruach* in Hebrew, *pneuma* in Greek) has "breath" among its meanings. Scripture, too, is a product of the Holy Spirit, and its divine origin guarantees its truth and trustworthiness in all the affirmations that it makes.

Furthermore, God-breathed Scripture, says Paul, is given precisely for the purpose of functioning as a means of spiritual and vocational formation: it is "useful for teaching, rebuking, correcting and training in righteousness, so that the man of God may be thoroughly equipped for every good work" (3:16-17). And "man of God" on Paul's lips means "You, Timothy!" The apostle is not generalizing, but particularizing. "Man of God" was an Old Testament designation for a prophet, God's messenger; Paul applied it to Timothy directly in 1 Timothy 6:11, and here he uses it the same way, to remind Timothy that as one entrusted with the truth of the gospel he stands in the prophetic succession, where fidelity to the message given is virtue number one. Paul is thus telling Timothy: "God wrote the Scriptures for you as much as for anybody; he addresses them specifically to you, as he does to every reader of them; he wrote them of set purpose to shape you for the service he had in mind for you; he wants you to be faithful and fruitful as a minister of the gospel." And from that point Paul sweeps straight on to insist that Timothy must at all times express his continuing Bible-based conviction about Jesus by consistent, Bible-based proclamation of Jesus: "Preach the Word" (4:2), that is, proclaim the Christ of the Scriptures according to the Scriptures. So Timothy's ongoing ministry of the gospel must be his personal response to the charge, not only of Paul in this letter, but of God himself addressing Timothy throughout the biblical text.

In this passage Paul was speaking, of course, of what we call the Old Testament, which was all the Bible that he and Timothy had; but his reasoning applies to all Scripture as such, so when we relate it to ourselves we may properly extend it to cover the New Testament also and thus the whole Christian Bible.

Paul's words here might be said to present the Bible as a business letter, dealing with work to be done and what it may cost, and this is indeed one side of the truth. God is businesslike in choosing and training leaders and preparing them for their tasks; all Christian service is "the king's business" (Dan. 8:27); Timothy would have done well to admonish himself in writing, as did William Perkins the Puritan, "Thou art a minister of the Word: Mind thy business." But the other side of the truth is that, just as the Bible is not an open letter to people in general but a word of specific address to each particular reader, so it is not just a business letter but is also a love letter, one in which God's redeeming love, plus a loving invitation to avail oneself of love's gifts, is the focal theme.

We take love letters very seriously. We love to receive them, and they fascinate us. We read them over and over, trying to squeeze out of them the last drop of meaning that the lover who wrote them put into them. Sometimes the writer's words of love affect us so poignantly as to take our breath away. I am bold to tell you that if we read the Bible seriously as God's love letter, this will be our experience time and time again. Start now, and see if I am not right.

Four: A Listening Post

Fourth, think of the Bible as a *listening post*, where you go to hear the voice of God. This thought follows on from the last.

Listening posts have long been key items in spy stories, as perhaps they have been in the world of real espionage. They are the places where the hero (or villain) can listen in to the bug placed in the villain's (or hero's) hotel room, or get a message on a private telephone which nobody knows about except himself. In describing the Holy Scripture as a listening post, I am pointing to its instrumentality as the means whereby we are enabled to understand the mind of God toward us, as I have been assuming all along that we actually can do. That is what I want to speak about now.

The key truth here is that our hearing of the specific things God has to say to us at this moment begins with our overhearing what he said to others long ago—to Abraham and Moses, for instance, by direct revelation, or to Israel via Moses and the prophets, or to the Romans or Corinthians or Philippians via the apostle Paul. In the Psalter we overhear David and others at prayer; in the Gospels we overhear Jesus talking to his disciples and to the Pharisees and to the woman at the well and to many others besides, in addition to overhearing his own prayers on a number of occasions. All this material is normative, one way or another, for forming our idea of the nature and character of God and coming to understand his will, work, and ways, his purposes, proposals, and principles of judgment and action. We saw earlier that from one standpoint, that of telling God's story, the narratives of Scripture are the backbone to which all the didactic revelations from God and about God are attached: from the present standpoint, however, that of grasping God's mind, God's messages are the backbone (think of them as so many vertebrae, all joined by the spinal cord of God's comprehensive cosmic plan and purpose), and the narratives of divine action in creation or control whereby God has fulfilled his word all come in as indicators of the real meaning of the messages themselves. As we watch God dealing with his world and with particular people in it, according to his words of purpose and promise, or of warning and threat, the significance of those words becomes plain, and increasingly we overhear with understanding. At our listening post we listen, we hear, and we learn.

As we have already noted, the Bible must be interpreted rightly if we are truly to hear its message. Just as in the spy stories you cannot hear anything intelligible if the phone in your listening post is being scrambled, so you will not get an accurate grasp of God's mind from a Bible that is being misinterpreted. About this, however, our present discussion requires us to say only two things.

Interpretation through the text itself. My first comment is that on the face of it the Bible is self-interpreting. Every one of its 66 books, we may confidently say, was written to be understood by its own first readers, and that means that we can understand it, too, just as we can understand the secular classics written in Latin and Greek. As with the classics, so with the Bible: every now and then we need to have a bit of historical background filled in for us, or we shall get hold of the wrong end of the stick. But most of the time these documents, being written by persons with hearts and minds like ours, yield up their meaning to anyone who reads them with ordinary care. Even enigmatic books like the visionary sections of Daniel and Revelation, which seem to us to be written in code, made sense to their original readers; they are in fact written in an idiom called "apocalyptic," a highly imaginative, imagistic, symbolic style that had been developed for dramatizing the conflict between God and chaotic tyrannical evil. The apocalyptic idiom of these books was well understood by their original readers and is well explained in present-day commentaries. The wise traveler, heading for foreign parts, reckons at least to buy a phrase book and start learning the lingo, and those who want to explore the exotic portions of Daniel and Revelation would be well advised to behave similarly—though it should be said that the exotic visions in both books are only orchestrating and reinforcing the essential lessons taught in Daniel 1–6 and Revelation 1–3. Most of the time, however, the Bible is written in ordinary, straightforward language with a clear, logical flow; the big and central things that it has to teach us are repeated and presented over and over in many different ways; and the sixty-six books are constantly throwing light on each other. So anyone who declares the Bible to be obscure is in fact bearing witness either to ignorance of the text or to some sort of blockage in the mind. There is nothing intrinsically puzzling about the Bible as a whole.

In pre-Reformation days the leaders of the Western church thought it a dreadful thing to let ordinary laypeople read the Bible. Such readers, they thought, were bound to get things wrong and end up challenging the church for not endorsing their own mistakes. The Bible was held to be a very difficult book, which none could properly understand without official guidance, and the Lollards, John Wycliffe's followers who treasured their vernacular Bible and affirmed the supremacy of Scripture and the right of all to read and interpret it for themselves, were actively persecuted as heretics. Against this the Reformers declared, over and over: "If you find the Bible difficult, the darkness is not in the Word, but in you. You need to go to God and acknowledge that sin has blinded your mind, and ask him to remove that blindness and enable you to see what is plain and clear in the pages of God's book." Surely they were right; and surely the encouragement that following Vatican II, four centuries later, the Roman Catholic leadership has begun to give its laity to read their Bibles is a very happy step forward.

Interpretation through the Christian heritage. My second comment is that on the face of it interpreters of Scripture should be aware of, and attuned to, the church's heritage of biblical study and exposition. For almost 2000 years the Holy Spirit has been teaching God's people truth and wisdom from the Scriptures, and it would be both ungrateful and stupid to ignore these resources. Did you know that Augustine and Chrysostom in the fifth century were fine biblical preachers? that Luther and Calvin and their peers established modern standards of biblical exposition? and that Calvin's commentaries on most of the Bible are of a quality that keeps him up with the leaders in the world of biblical scholarship today? Did you know that Matthew Henry's commentary on the whole Bible (nearly 300 years old, and still in print) skims the cream off more than a century of deep biblical exposition by Puritan writers? that first-class biblical elucidations fill the pages of theologians like John Owen, Jonathan Edwards, John Wesley, Charles Hodge, and Gerrit Berkouwer? and that more reverent, scholarly, well-informed and reliable commentaries and commentary series are in print today for English readers than were available in any previous generation? Do you know how wide is the range of biblical truth that the currently available sermons of men like Charles Spurgeon and Martyn Lloyd-Jones, and books by men such as Arthur Pink, John Stott, R. C. Sproul and James Montgomery Boice actually cover, crystallize, predigest, and bring down to earth for us? The resources are vast, and the extent to which they mesh in with each other is amazing; why then do we not make more use of them?

There is, of course, nothing infallible about any tradition of teaching; intellectual sanctification is no more perfect in this life than its moral counterpart is, and anyone who is usually right can still be wrong about this or that particular item. All expositions of Scripture must finally be tested by the Scriptures they seek to expound; the Bible must always have the last word. But anyone who ignores the help in understanding that this rich heritage can give is bound to end up with an unduly narrow, and perhaps actually eccentric, view of many things. And that will be, to say the least, a pity.

Problems have been created among God's people from the first by men and women whom we may fitly describe as the Pied Pipers of religion: magnetic, confident, masterful teachers who appeal to the Bible but whose expositions are eccentric. The pattern is familiar. They claim superior enlightenment; they gain a following of captivated admirers who treat them as virtually infallible; they found their own organizations, associations, and churches; they dismiss corrective criticism as intellectually perverse, spiritually second-rate, and not worth bothering with; and they lead many out of the Christian mainstream into a closed-off, sectarian way of life. A recent example was the first half-century of the Worldwide Church of God, founded and run by Herbert W. Armstrong on an anti-Trinitarian, anti-Christendom, Anglo-Israelite, Saturday-Sabbath, Jewish-festival-calendar, end-times-oriented, prediction-focused reading of the Bible, largely legalistic and shackled to pre-Christian patterns of life. Unusually for a body of this type, after Armstrong's death in 1986 there was a total rethinking, and the WCG has been led by the Bible's own self-interpretation, which its ongoing leadership could no longer negate, to become a generically evangelical Protestant community, living, as its own spokesmen now insist, under God's new covenant in and through our Lord Jesus Christ. (Ruth Tucker tells the story in *Christianity Today*, 15 July 1996.) But most groups with Pied Piper origins continue as they began—or, at least, claim to be continuing as they began, according to the direction set by their founder(s), never mind what actual changes may in fact be made as they move along. The Mormons and Jehovah's Witnesses are examples of this. Such is the unhappy legacy of the Pied Pipers, who decline to get help in their own biblical understanding from the church's heritage of biblical faith.

The paragraphs above would be misunderstood, however, if they were read as an attempt to discourage believers from reading and re-reading the text of Scripture as such, as if reading other people's expositions would be a better option. Some, indeed, do in fact follow the path of reading only what others say that the Bible says—and they lose by it. Those who regularly read the text itself, seeking always to know God better and to grow in the saving grace of Jesus Christ, find that again and again biblical statements leap out at them and speak to their hearts as from God directly. Within the limits and outlook established by the "fly-on-the-wall" method of interpretation that was described above, those who approach the Bible as their listening post and listen for God as they read it really do hear the divine voice. (I mean, they are made aware of particular things that God is saying to them about his relationship with them and their relationship with him.) Which leads us on to the next point in our analysis of the Christian way of approaching the Bible.

Five: A Law

Fifth, be clear that Holy Scripture, which, as we have already seen, comes to us from God as a library, a landscape, a letter, and a listening post, is also a *law* for us—the law of God, which is his map of the ideal life, and as such his syllabus for the saints. This is law in the sense of the Hebrew word *torah:* that is, affectionate instruction on behavior as from a father to his family, given in the expectation that the children will take it to heart and faithfully obey their father's directives. Moderns, hearing the word *law,* at once think of the law of the land, a formidable set of requirements and restrictions put in place by remote bodies (Congress, Parliament, the Supreme Court) or by dictatorial governors with whom ordinary citizens have no direct links. The law of the Lord, however, differs from the law of the land—any land—in at least two major ways.

To start with, it contains more than bare formal requirements and restrictions; it includes promises alongside its precepts, and wisdom about life's meaning and purpose and about the plan and work of God, alongside both. *Torah* covers everything that God sees fit to tell us for his glory and our good, about creation and providence, about sin and salvation, about present pressures and future hopes, as well as about right and wrong ways of behaving. When we realize that all that is set forth in Scripture is God's *torah* and that the context of all his commandments is his covenant of grace, we can better understand why the psalmists say: "The law of the LORD is perfect, reviving the soul. . . . The precepts of the LORD are right, giving joy to the heart" (Ps. 19:7-8); and: "Oh, how I love your law! I meditate on it all day long" (Ps. 119:97; see also verses 47, 127, 163, 165); and: "Blessed is the man . . . [whose] delight is in the law of the LORD" (Ps. 1:1-2). May the fullness of this blessing become ours!

Then, secondly, as was said above, God gives his servants his law within a family frame. It was so when Moses, in his role as prophet—that is, spokesman for God, relaying revelation—first declared God's law to the Israelites; it came to them at Sinai from the God who had already taken them to be his family and had earlier sent Moses to say to Pharaoh: "Israel is my firstborn son, and I told you, 'Let my son go, so he may worship me'" (Exod. 4:22-23; see also Deut. 32:6; Is. 63:16, 64:8; Jer. 3:19, 31:9; Hos. 11:1; Mal. 2:10). It remains so under the New Testament order of things; thus, the Sermon on the Mount, in which Jesus appears as the new Moses restating God's *torah* for the kingdom era then beginning (God's new age, as we might call it), has at its heart the proclamation of God as heavenly Father of all Jesus' disciples. Matthew 6 contains a dozen explicit references to God as Father, and the child-Father relationship is the theme of the whole chapter. Pharisees and Judaizers seem to have thought of the law in its precepts and prohibitions as a means of winning God's favor on a merit basis, but both Testaments view it as a family code for those whom God has graciously taken into his favor and made his children already. Now, as God's covenant family, enjoying his pardon and peace, they must honor and glorify their heavenly Father by living to his praise, and God sets before them his *torah* to show them how this is to be done.

Earlier we saw that the backbone of the Bible is its history of redemption, on which hang all its teachings about worship, lifestyle, and service. When biblical behavior is our focus of inquiry, therefore, we should always interpret God's imperatives from within this framework. That means understanding them as pointing always to the ideal form of a believer's life, in which the basic reality is the desire to love, exalt, and glorify God for his mercy, and to please him by loving others for his sake, modeling towards them the love God has shown to oneself. Theological logic, therefore, leads us to conclude that biblical commandments mean not only "do this, and don't do that," which was all that the scribes and Pharisees thought they meant, but also "be (that is, become) the kind of person who does this and doesn't do that." This is a dimension of the law's meaning which the Jewish pundits seemed to miss entirely, but which Christians properly highlight whenever they speak of Jesus as the law incarnate and embodied and go on to proclaim the power of the Holy Spirit to transform believers into the Savior's image.

It needs to be said, before we move on, that living by biblical *torah* can be costly. Society will press Christians to do things that God's law forbids and to omit things that God's law requires. Christian nonconformity to others' ways will be felt as an insult and a threat. In the early centuries Christians were persecuted throughout the Roman empire because they would not join in Emperor-worship. Persecution is rife today in Muslim and Marxist countries where toleration is not part of the culture and Christians are seen as subversive of national goals. In the West, Christian physicians who will not do abortions are marginalized in their own profession, and in many circles Christians who still see homosexual practice as sin are, to say the least, very much disliked. Christians, however, must obey God rather than humans when there is a clash (see Acts 4:19, 5:29), and if that means trouble, so be it: we have to learn to commit our cause to God and stand steady, seeing the situation as a testing of our faith. But living by Scripture as one's law in this way can cost a great deal, and we must face that fact realistically.

Further, it needs to be said that living by biblical *torah* can be disturbing. It has been said that either the Bible will keep you from sin or sin will keep you from the Bible.

What is meant is that the Bible will jolt us to the roots of our being by zeroing in on our weaknesses, shortcomings, vices, disobediences, and neglects, and will sensitize our consciences to the displeasure of God and the imperative need to make changes. At such times we shall find that the temptation to stop taking the Bible seriously will be very strong indeed. Jesus pictures the price that the changes may involve by speaking of the cutting off of a hand or foot or the gouging out of one's eye (Matt. 5:29-30; Mark 9:43-48): he is envisaging action which in prospect looks like a diminishing of one's life. The renouncing of addictive sin always appears like this. That the fruit of such renouncing is a truer freedom and a larger life is something we do not discover till we have taken the plunge and done it, looking to God to enable us to maintain our decision once we have made it. C. S. Lewis illustrates this unforgettably in his fantasy *The Great Divorce,* where the lizard of lust sits on a wraith's shoulder telling him he cannot live without it while an angel asks leave to kill it; and once the wraith consents and it is killed, there is a transforming resurrection whereby wraith and lizard become rider and horse, galloping glory-wards. The resurrection-out-of-death principle that flows from Calvary guarantees that all the renouncings of evil for which Scripture calls will sooner or later bring enrichment of life. But, as Lewis makes a point of showing, the renouncing may hurt acutely at the time of doing it, and the battle for obedience may be far from easy to win.

Also it needs to be said that living by biblical *torah* can be very humbling. Pride is the sinful infection of all our hearts, and we are all proud to a degree of our opinions.

But if as we let Scripture instruct us we find it teaching something different from what we have hitherto assumed, and contradicting what, as we say, we "like to think" (ominous phrase!), then it is so much the worse for our former thoughts, and we have to change our minds. To admit that you were wrong can be painful; but those who take Scripture as law for their lives must be prepared for this.

Six: A Light

Sixth, always approach Holy Scripture as Psalm 119:105 in effect directs when it says: "Your word is a lamp to my feet and a light for my path." See in your mind's eye the picture; never get away from it. You have to take a journey across open country, and it is dark. Traveling in the dark across open country—rough country, too—you are at risk. The easiest thing in the world will be to lose the path, stumble and fall over some obstacle that in the dark you could not see, and do yourself serious mischief. The likelihood of your reaching your destination in the dark is small. However much you screw up your eyes and glare into the blackness, you are still unable to see the way to go. There is a path—you know that—but without a light you cannot hope to keep to it. You need a light (it was oil lamps in the ancient world, but think of a flashlight as what you need today)—and God in his mercy puts one into your hand. You shine it in front of you, and you can see the next bit of the track, so that step by step you know where to put your foot. You walk without stumbling; you follow the path; you move ahead towards your goal. "Your word is a lamp to my feet and a light for my path."

One of the museums of biblical archaeology, so I am told, displays a little oil lamp made with a hook in its base so that it cannot stand upright. Archaeologists puzzled for some time over it until someone saw that the purpose of the hook must have been to fasten the lamp to the strap of a sandal, so that the traveler would have his lamp at his feet—actually on his foot—to guide his steps through the dark. Exactly! That is the psalmist's picture to perfection.

What does the picture mean? It means that a Christian can always find in the Bible guidance as to the next step in obedience, whatever perplexities his or her life situation may currently present. Walking by the light of Scripture is not like walking by daylight, any more than shining your flashlight is like the rising of the sun. Beyond the little circle of vision that your flashlight gives you, the darkness remains, and it is through this continuing darkness that you travel. You are regularly in the dark, in the everyday slang sense, unable to find meaning in the things that happen around you. But Scripture enables you to see each next step that you must take, so on you are able to go.

All of us, I am bold to say, walk through life with a quiverful of unanswered questions about the ways of God. Why this? Why that? What is really going on here? We don't know, for God does not tell us. All he tells us, as we consult his Word, is how to cope Christianly with this and that as it comes and to get on with our life of worship and service through it all. You may find yourself similarly placed when you drive a car. You cannot imagine why so many people on the road behave in such strange ways. But you know the principles of watching for hazards, taking avoiding action, and driving correctly despite the oddities of other motorists' behavior, and so you are able to move along despite everything. The Bible leads us across the rough country of life in a comparable way, not giving us answers to all the theoretical questions we like to ask (Did God create life on other planets? Why did God allow the Holocaust? Will anyone be saved without knowing about Jesus Christ? and so on), but enabling us to follow the path of fidelity, wisdom, and righteousness as Jesus and Paul and so many more did before us. We must learn to come to Scripture in that healthy state of mind in which we have given up on our own wisdom and are vividly conscious of needing light from God to guide us through life's problems. A sense of one's own inner darkness and need of God's illuminating instruction is the best possible preparation for exploring one's Bible and discovering what it has to say to you—that is, what light God has to give you through it—at each point in life's journey. I try to maintain that sense, and I hope you do too.

A very striking New Testament passage makes a point parallel to that of the psalm, namely 2 Peter 1:19-21. Having referred to his experience on the Mount of Transfiguration as warrant for his assertion that what he had taught about "the power and coming of our Lord Jesus Christ" was fact, not fantasy, Peter moves on to say, literally in the Greek: "And we have something surer, the prophetic word (of the Old Testament)." Most commentators and all modern translators take this to mean that Peter's experience of seeing Jesus' glory confirmed the prophetic word about him, written centuries before. But since Peter says "surer" (adjective), not "confirmed" (passive participle), and since the current Jewish view was that prophecy was always more reliable than any vision or voice from heaven, it is better to take Peter as saying in effect: "The prophetic Scriptures are surer than any experience I have to share, so I appeal to those Scriptures to confirm what I have just told you." This is right in line with the very strong assertion that Peter takes time out to make in verse 21—"prophecy never had its origin in the will of man, but men spoke from God as they were carried along by the Holy Spirit." Note now his statement about the prophetic word of Scripture in the second half of verse 19—"you will do well to pay attention to it, as to a light shining in a dark place, until the day dawns and the morning star rises in your hearts." The word for "dark" implies murky and messy. Peter identifies as the fallen human heart the dark place where the day must dawn (that is, where firm conviction about "the *power* and *coming* of our Lord Jesus Christ," in other words his divinity, mediatorial role and reign, present requirements of moral and spiritual advance, and future return to judgment needs to be established). It is there that murk and mess are found, in the form of unbelief, misbelief, uncertainty, bewilderment, confusion, apathy, and distortion, not only about the person and place of Jesus but also about the Christian way to live (see chapters 2 and 3 of Peter's letter), and there that the light of Scripture needs to shine to give clarity, stability, and discernment of the proper path. So— "pay attention to it!" Let the light do its work!

Seven: A Lifeline

Is it fanciful and strained to affirm that the seventh category for our approach to Holy Scripture should be that of a lifeline? I do not think so. A lifeline is a rope to which a drowning person clings while being pulled ashore. Drowning is a condition of being invaded and overwhelmed by water, which gets into your lungs so that you cannot breathe. Metaphorically, you can be said to drown in sorrow, or grief, or any other invasive mood that disrupts normal personal life. Now, we are surrounded today by people who are drowning inwardly in the raging waters of hopelessness. The proverb rightly says that while there's life there's hope, but the deeper truth is that only while there's hope is there life: When the light of hope goes out, and there really seems nothing to live for anymore, life itself becomes a killing burden. We are so made that we live very much in our future, and the desolation of feeling that there is nothing worthwhile to come, nothing good ever to be expected again, eats the soul away like a corrosive acid. To moderns drowning in hopelessness, disappointed, disillusioned, despairing, emotionally isolated, bitter and aching inside, Bible truth comes as a lifeline, for it is future-oriented and hope-centered throughout. The God of the Bible, whom Christians know as the Father, the Son, and the Holy Spirit united in a shared divine life, is both a very present help in trouble and a very potent hope in times of despair. The triune God, we might say, is the lifeguard, who comes in person to the place where we are drowning in order to rescue us; the Holy Scriptures are the lifeline God throws us in order to ensure that he and we stay connected while the rescue is in progress; and the hope that the Scriptures bring us arrests and reverses the drowning experience here and now, generating inward vitality and renewed joy and banishing forever the sense of having the life choked out of us as the waves break over us.

That the Bible throughout is a book of hope is not always appreciated, but it is so. From the giving of the promise that the woman's seed will crush the serpent's head (Gen. 3:15), the Old Testament constantly looks forward to great restorative things that God will do for his people and his world. The New Testament nails down this hope by its repeated assurances that the Lord Jesus Christ, our divine Sin-bearer and present heavenly Friend, is with us by his Spirit to keep us sane and safe till he returns to re-create the cosmos and lead us all into unimaginable endless glory with himself. Meantime, he gives our lives permanent and satisfying meaning by making us his servants, with jobs to do, and that is a relationship that will continue forever. In a world in which the individual's natural sense of significance is so largely snuffed out, such a hope is a lifeline indeed.

The deep-level story of the twentieth century is of hope destroyed. In 1900 the hope was that this would be "the Christian century" (title of a liberal Christian periodical that was founded to chart its course). The twentieth century was expected to see unprecedented Christian advance. The church would spread, the ethnic religions would crumble, all humankind would be Christianized, and the kingdom of God would come on earth. These hopes failed to reckon with the titanic energy of human sin and the spiritual shortcomings of liberal Christianity and have come to nothing. What has happened is the opposite of what was looked for. Our century has seen two nightmarish world wars, each followed by a spectacular failure to win the peace and make militarism a thing of the past.

Wars continue. Meanwhile, Christianity in all its forms has lost its grip on the West, which now leads the world in materialistic, relativistic, and hedonistic secularization. The size of its arms industry is the measure of its cynicism; the size of its abortion industry is the measure of its paganism. The global culture that has established itself is not a Christian ideology but a technological monster, raping the planet for financial profit and generating horrendous ecological prospects for our grandchildren. The great Asian religions, Hinduism, Buddhism, and Islam, have come to new life to oppose global Christianity. Our era has turned into an age of atrocity, in which the barbarian obscenities of terrorism, genocide, torture, and religious and political persecution have re-established themselves on a grander scale than ever before. The prospectus of an overseas hotel catering to English-speaking tourists declared: "Our wines leave you nothing to hope for"—a classic example of not saying quite what you mean, so that your words become a joke. But anyone who said that our century leaves us nothing to hope for would undoubtedly be expressing exactly what was meant, and what was meant would be true, and the very opposite of a joke. At such a time the Bible's message of personal and cosmic hope beyond the present order of things is a lifeline for us indeed.

Scripture and Hope

Four and a half centuries ago Archbishop Thomas Cranmer and his colleagues, discerning the crucial link between Scripture and hope, composed for the Anglican Prayer Book the following petition:

Blessed Lord, who hast caused all holy scriptures to be written for our learning; Grant that we may in such wise hear them, read, mark, learn, and inwardly digest them, that by patience, and comfort of thy holy Word, we may embrace, and ever hold fast the blessed hope of everlasting life, which thou hast given us in our Saviour Jesus Christ.

Several points should be noted with regard to this prayer.

First, it is set for use each second Sunday in Advent, when Romans 15:4-13 is the New Testament epistle reading that follows it. It echoes the epistle; it is in fact the message of the epistle distilled into petitionary form. This demonstrates to us the right use of the Bible in the devotional life. God's Word comes to us so that we may know how to speak our word to him. God approaches us humans in and by his Word, disclosing himself there; we worshipers take that word of revelation and turn it into praise, prayer, and adoration as we approach God in response. Christian prayer in essence is never blind groping, but always builds intelligently on what God himself says.

Second, the prayer echoes 2 Timothy 3:16 as well as Romans 15:4 in affirming that *all* Holy Scripture has in the providence of God been written for our learning—learning, that is, on the part of every congregation and individual in any and every age. So, in the life both of the church and of the individual, the whole Bible is to be used. We all tend to limit our Bible reading to our own favorite passages or books, and this can lead to inadequate views of God and unbalanced spiritual development. At one time many Christians possessed a promise box, packed with divine promises from Scripture on separate slips of paper, to be drawn out at random as a kind of pick-me-up when inspiration and encouragement were felt to be needed. So far, so good; but should these saints not also have had a precept box, or even a threat box, beside their promise box to counterbalance this one-sided practice? In any case, boxed texts cannot set before us anything like the full sweep of Scripture. Nor should we restrict our biblical diet, as some do, to a few familiar psalms and the four Gospels. No doubt there is in any one of these portions of Holy Writ more than we shall ever fathom, but we are less likely to plumb their depths if we isolate them from the rest of God's revelation. By all means let us read and re-read our favorite passages as often as we want to, but all Scripture should be regularly read as well.

Third, this prayer tells us that we who are literate should not only *read* Scripture for ourselves as well as hear it read in church, but should *mark, learn,* and *inwardly digest* it. A progression of intensity in application is being outlined here. We are to read Scripture attentively and retentively. Learning by rote—that is, memorizing—has gone out of fashion, but we can hardly afford to do without it. Bishop Nicholas Ridley, one of the English Reformation martyrs, looked back to the days when

> I learned without book almost all Paul's epistles. . . . Of which study, although in time a great part did depart from me, yet the sweet smell thereof I trust I shall carry into heaven; for the profit thereof I think I have felt in all my life time ever after.

Marking and learning the Scriptures (that is, taking full note of them and appreciating their full weight) requires some form of memorization; then masticating them (the first step towards inwardly digesting them) requires meditation (probing imagination, prayerful reflection, and personal application); and absorbing them into one's spiritual system requires appetite—a constant craving to know God and his truth.

Addictive drugs stimulate the appetite they satisfy in a way that undermines character, producing instability and desensitizing conscience. The Holy Scriptures, by contrast, stimulate the appetite they satisfy in a way that fortifies character, producing a concentrated focus on seeking God's highest and best. It is a striking fact of Christian experience everywhere that the Bible feeds not only the hungry heart but the hunger itself, constantly increasing our appetite to know more of God and hence our passion to dig more deeply into his Word. We see this in the psalmist, to whom God's words were sweeter than honey (Ps. 119:103), and whose longing for God's commandments—that is, for insight into them and fulfilment of them—nagged at his heart as hunger and thirst nag at our bodily consciousness (see vv. 18, 20, 123, 131).

Fourth, the prayer tells us that "comfort" from Scripture sustains Christians in their hope that unfailing present grace will lead them on to unfading eternal glory. "Comfort" here carries the old, strong, sixteenth-century, King-James-Version sense drawn from the Latin verb *confortare*, which means "make strong." Comfort of this sort is not the soothing that ends tension and makes you relax, but the strengthening that comes from encouragement that energizes and puts new heart into you. The Bayeux tapestry celebrating the Norman conquest of England depicts King Harold urging his troops forward at the Battle of Hastings, and *confortat* (comforts!) is the verb used in the caption. *Encouragement*, the majority rendering in twentieth-century versions of the English Bible, is the word that best expresses what Paul meant when in Romans 15:4 he wrote of the *paraklesis* of the Scripture, and also what Cranmer meant when he echoed this phrase in the prayer, using *comfort* for the purpose.

To illustrate the power of Scripture as a lifeline that sustains hope, let me be autobiographical for a moment. I do not think of my experience as having any special significance except to me, but I would like to share it because it happened. For fifteen years I worked to fulfill a vision of evangelical quickening in England through theological education, spiritual formation, pastoral enrichment, profound preaching, wise evangelism, functional Christian unity, and every-member ministry in local congregations—a vision generated by the type of pure biblical theology that some label Puritan Calvinism. Put like that, of course, this vision sounds grandiose to a fault, and though I retain my hold on it—or, rather, it retains its hold on me—I am not here concerned to defend it against its critics. I simply record that after fifteen years of actively promoting it came several years during which, through what people with other visions did in perfectly good faith to block, more or less directly, the things I was after, I lost all the vantage-points I had had for implementing the purposes that the vision dictated. I found myself marginalized, isolated, and required to work to unfulfilling and, I thought, flawed agendas, in a manner that made me think of the Israelites having to make bricks for Pharaoh; and for political reasons I was not free to say what I thought about this state of affairs. Outwardly appreciated, at least by some, as a useful Christian performer, I lived, like Moses in Midian, with frustration in my heart, wondering what God, who as I believed gave the vision in the first place, could possibly be up to. The Bible, however, kept assuring me that God knows his business, so even though I expected to soldier on where I was till retirement I had hope.

During those years my spiritual education was proceeding. Here are the main lessons that God through his Word hammered into my heart.

(1) Goodwill—I should not get bitter or lapse into self-pity or spend time complaining or angling for sympathy. God was using my ministry and I was forbidden to get fixated on my frustrations.

(2) Hope—I was not to become cynical or apathetic about the vision I had been given or to abandon it because there was no immediate way of advancing it. God is never in a hurry, and waiting in hope is a Christian discipline.

(3) Faithfulness—As husband, father, teacher, honorary assistant pastor, and occasional author, I had plenty each day to get on with, and I could not honor God by slackness and negligence, whatever discontents I was carrying around inside me.

(4) Compassion—Clearly I was being taught to empa-

thize more deeply with the many Christians, lay and ordained, male and female, who live with various kinds of disappointments and thus were in the same boat as myself.

(5) Humility—I must never forget that God is supreme and important, and I am neither, and he can manage very well without me whenever he chooses to do so.

God alone knows how far I managed to live out these lessons, but there was no lack of clarity as he presented them to me from the Scriptures.

In due course things changed. With clear guidance from inner conviction and outward circumstances, both biblically judged, my wife and I emigrated, and today I follow the gleam of the original vision of reformation and revival in a larger world than England. Tabasco sauce (often imitated, never duplicated, as its labels say) gains its flavor from the oak barrels in which it matures. I suspect that those final years in England were a sort of oak barrel period for me, but I leave that for others to decide.

There are many things about my life that I do not know and do not expect to know till the books are opened. The mother of a school friend was clairvoyant, though as a Christian she wished she was not, and in any case she was not always able to tell her genuine second sight from her own wishful thinking. Before I was a believer she surprised and, I confess, amused me by assuring me that I would end up in the Christian ministry. I remember her also admonishing me in those far-off days that I should need to remember the proverbial wisdom that Kipling versified in

the line: "he travels the fastest who travels alone." Her first
word was verified; whether the second has been I cannot
tell as yet. But I have totally verified the wisdom of David's
words in Psalm 27:14—"Wait for the LORD; be strong and
take heart and wait for the LORD"—and so far as ongoing
hope is concerned, truths I keep meeting in Scripture have
taken me back over and over again before, during, and
since the years of frustration, to words of Anna Waring that
have been in my heart since I learned them as a student
more than fifty years ago:

> In heavenly love abiding
> No change my heart shall fear;
> And safe is such confiding,
> For nothing changes here.
> The storm may roar without me,
> My heart may low be laid;
> But God is round about me:
> And can I be dismayed?
>
> Wherever he may guide me
> No want shall turn me back;
> My shepherd is beside me,
> And nothing can I lack;
> His wisdom ever waketh,
> His sight is never dim;
> He knows the way he taketh,
> And I will walk with him.
>
> Green pastures are before me,
> Which yet I have not seen;

Bright skies will soon be o'er me
Where the dark clouds have been.
My hope I cannot measure,
My path to life is free;
My Savior has my treasure,
And he will walk with me.

The Bible a lifeline? It has certainly been so for me, and I hope it will prove itself similarly so for everyone who ever reads this book.

A Most Precious Thing

I often make reference in public to the words set to be spoken by the Moderator of the Church of Scotland in the British Coronation service as he hands the new monarch the Bible. He calls it "the most valuable thing that this world affords, . . . wisdom . . . the royal law . . . the lively oracles of God." The goal of this book has been to confirm that estimate and to bring my readers to the point at which, with John Newton, their hearts say:

Precious Bible! what a treasure
  Does the Word of God afford!
All I want for life or pleasure,
  Food and medicine, shield and sword;
Let the world account me poor—
Christ and this, I need no more.

Those who have reached this point will also find their hearts saying, with John Burton:

Holy Bible, Book divine!
Precious treasure, thou art mine!
Mine, to tell me whence I came;
Mine, to teach me what I am.

Mine, to chide me when I rove;
Mine, to show a Savior's love;
Mine art thou, to guide my feet;
Mine, to judge, condemn, acquit.

Mine, to comfort in distress,
Mine, with promise sweet to bless;
Mine, to show by living faith
Man can triumph over death.

Mine, to tell of joys to come;
Mine, to show the sinner's doom;
Holy Bible, Book divine!
Precious treasure, thou art mine!

Though not outstanding as poetry, these verses of Newton and Burton are outstanding expressions of the Bible-moth Christianity that I write to advocate. Bible-moth Christianity is, so I urge, the truest, deepest, strongest sort of Christianity, the sort that knows most about the supernatural life into which the new birth brings us and the sort that has most power to stand against the onrush of secularity that we face today. Western Christianity has become superficial and shallow: we do not give ourselves time to soak ourselves in Scripture, and stunted spiritual development, which includes an undervaluing of the Bible, is the unhappy result. We need to be clear that, other things being equal, it is the Bible-moth Christians, who eat up the Scriptures on a regular basis, who are likely to achieve most for our Lord Jesus Christ in the future, just as it was Bible-moth Christians who achieved most for him in the past.

Shall we see in these days a return to Bible-moth Christianity, in which the precious treasure of God's written Word is honored for what it is and used as it should be for life, and health, and peace? As Martin Luther King had his dream of an America freed from racism, so I have my dream of Christianity freed from relativism, scepticism, anti-intellectualism, and anti-biblicism: a Christianity whose adherents are all learning to testify to the truth and power of the Scriptures, and to stand together to proclaim biblical truth as it is in Jesus. I believe I have seen something of this already, in the very remarkable worldwide evangelical advance during the past half-century; shall I see any more of it in my lifetime? I do not know. But God is on the throne, and I have hope in him.

Meantime, I am thankful for this opportunity of showing the world how excited I am about the Scriptures, and of sharing my enthusiasm as I have been doing. God grant to all my readers a share of that same excitement and a full measure of that divine life in Christ to which love for God's written Word opens the door.

ENDNOTES

Chapter 2/FORMED, DEFORMED, REFORMED

1. J. I. Packer, *"Fundamentalism" and the Word of God* (London: Inter-Varsity Press and Grand Rapids, Mich.: Eerdmans, 1958), pp. 152ff. See also James Barr, *The Bible in the Modern World* (London: SCM Press, 1973), pp. 1-12; and Brevard S. Childs, *Biblical Theology in Crisis* (Philadelphia: Westminster Press, 1970), pp. 13-87, 103-4: Childs's footnotes are in effect a superb bibliography of the "biblical theology" movement from the North American perspective. Cf. J. D. Smart, *The Past, Present and Future of Biblical Theology* (Philadelphia: Westminster Press, 1979).

2. Packer, *"Fundamentalism" and the Word of God*, p. 158.

3. Cf. Childs, *Biblical Theology in Crisis*, pp. 51-87. Barr, *The Bible in the Modern World*, p. 10, classifies the questions which "biblical theology" is nowadays felt to have left unanswered as follows:

(i) Questions about *relevance* . . . how . . . can material from that very different biblical situation be decisive for our problems?

(ii) Questions about *communicability* . . . how . . . can we expect what was meaningful to [the men of the Bible] to communicate the same meaning to us?

(iii) Questions about *limitations:* The Bible is a limited set of books, chosen partly by accident and coming from a limited segment of the total history of the church; how can its insights be decisive for us in any way which is qualitatively different from that which attaches to other books and other times?

(iv) Questions about *isolation:* How can the Bible be assigned a position qualitatively different from all the other factors which come into the mind . . . when decisions about faith and ethics have to be taken?

(v) Questions about *our responsibility:* The task of the church is to say what the church and Christians believe today. This responsibility is evaded or distorted if we suppose that our main responsibility is to restate, to reinterpret, or to make our thoughts dependent upon, what was believed by the men of biblical times.

Barr's summary is as precise as it is provocative.

4. The "canonical" approach of Brevard S. Childs, as seen in his *Commentary on Exodus*, Old Testament Library (Philadelphia: Westminster Press, 1974), and his *Introduction to the Old Testament as Scripture* (Philadelphia: Fortress Press, 1979), seems to me a very important step in the right direction, though Childs might not agree with my statement in the text.

5. See chapter 4, below, where this approach to biblical interpretation is more fully analyzed.

6. See J. R. Gieselmann, "Scripture, Tradition and the Church: an Ecumenical Problem" in *Christianity Divided*, ed. by D. J. Callahan, H. A. Obermann, and D. J. O'Hanlon (London: Sheed & Ward, 1962), pp. 39ff. Trent said that gospel doctrine is given us in written books and *(et)* unwritten traditions. The Council agreed on the noncommittal "et" as an alternative to a proposal to say that doctrine comes to us partly in the Scriptures and partly in unwritten traditions *(partim . . . partim . . .)*; thus it was left open to regard the traditions as expository of rather than supplementary to what is written.

7. "Constitution on Revelation," II.7-10, in *The Documents of Vatican II*, ed. by Walter M. Abbott (London: Geoffrey Chapman; and New York: The America Press and Association Press, 1966), pp. 114-18; also in *Vatican II: Conciliar and Post-conciliar Documents*, ed. by Austin P. Flannery (Grand Rapids, Mich.: Eerdmans, 1975), pp. 753-56.

8. In his article, "Biblical Theology" in *Lexicon für Theologie und Kirche*, vol. 2, ed. by J. Hofer and K. Rahner (Freiburg: Verlag Herder, 1958), pp. 449-50, Rahner affirms that the proclamation of the church's faith must be founded on Scripture, as the basis of authority for faith and life, and that Scripture stands above tradition as the only *norma non normanda* [standard not subject to another standard], and that nothing should be held and taught in the church that is not motivated and sanctioned by Scripture.

9. See the report, "Tradition and Traditions," in *Faith and Order Findings*, ed. by Paul S. Minear (London: SCM Press, 1963); also, Max Thurian, *Visible Unity and Tradition* (London: Darton, Longman & Todd, 1964), with the bibliographical notes on p. 53.

10. "Recommendations for Diocesan Ecumenical Commissions," circulated by the Roman Catholic Ecumenical Commission for England and Wales and dated May 1968 called for the forming of house groups of Roman Catholics and others who would "start by discussing what various Christian traditions have in common" and go on "to pray together, and to join in Bible study." Roman Catholics were to "take the initiative in starting such groups, in the conviction that they have much to give, though also something to learn" (p. 16).

11. G. B. Bentley, *The Resurrection of the Bible* (London: Dacre Press, 1940), p.1.

12. New York: Doubleday, and Harmondsworth: Penguin, 1957. See also G. Hebert, *The Bible from Within* (London: Oxford Univ. Press, 1950); "The Holy Bible: Its Authority and Message" in *The Lambeth Conference, 1958* (London:

SPCK, 1958), 2.1ff.; H. H. Rowley, *The Rediscovery of the Bible* (London: Hodder & Stoughton, 1954); etc.

13. See B. B. Warfield, "God-inspired Scripture," *The Works of Benjamin B. Warfield*, vol. 1 of *Revelation and Inspiration* (Grand Rapids, Mich.: Baker Book House, 1981), pp. 245-96—an article dating from 1900, but still definitive.

14. See C. H. Dodd, *According to the Scriptures* (London: Nisbet, 1952); R. V. G. Tasker, *The Old Testament in the New Testament*, 2nd ed. (London: SCM Press, 1954); E. Earle Ellis, *Paul's Use of the Old Testament* (Edinburgh: Oliver & Boyd, 1957); B. Lindars, *New Testament Apologetic* (London: SCM Press, 1961); F. F. Bruce, *This Is That* (Exeter: Paternoster Press, 1968); etc.

15. Article, "Inspiration" in *The New Bible Dictionary*, ed. J. D. Douglas *et al.* (London: Inter-Varsity Fellowship, 1962), p. 564.

16. *pulchra omnium partium inter se consensio (Institutio* I. viii. 1).

17. See R. E. Davies, *The Problem of Authority in the Continental Reformers* (London: Epworth Press, 1946), pp. 114 ff.; E. A. Dowey, *The Knowledge of God in Calvin's Theology* (New York: Columbia Univ. Press, 1952), pp. 101 ff.; John Murray, *Calvin on Scripture and Divine Sovereignty* (Philadelphia: Presbyterian and Reformed Publishing, n.d.), chapters 1 and 2; J. I. Packer, "Calvin the Theologian" in *John Calvin*, ed. G. E. Duffield (Abingdon: Sutton Courtenay Press, 1966), pp. 162 ff.; "Calvin's Doctrine of Scripture" in ed. J. W. Montgomery, *God's Inerrant Word*, (Minneapolis: Bethany Press, 1974, pp. 95 ff.; and "John Calvin and the Inerrancy of Holy Scripture," in *Inerrancy and the Church*, ed. J. Hannah (Chicago: Moody Press, 1984), pp. 143 ff.; H. J. Forstman, *Word and Spirit* (Stanford: Stanford Univ. Press, 1962), pp. 49 ff.

18. Abbott, *Documents of Vatican II*, pp. 118-21; Flannery, *Vatican II*, pp. 756-58.

19. "The statement, like so many others at the Council, is a compromise. It is deliberately ambiguous so that the old and the new views of the Bible can alike appeal to it. But Rome had not been ambiguous on this point before; therefore, it should be considered a victory for the progressives" (Clark Pinnock in Montgomery, ed., *God's Inerrant Word*, p. 147; cf. Montgomery, *God's Inerrant Word*, pp. 263ff.).

20. John A. T. Robinson's important volume, *Redating the New Testament* (London: SCM Press, 1976), shows that it is not necessary to posit a date later than A.D. 70 for any New Testament book.

21. For a survey of the very little information about Jesus that can be gleaned extra-biblically, see Roderic Dunkerley, *Beyond the Gospels* (Harmondsworth: Penguin, 1957); R. T. France, *The Evidence for Jesus* (Downers Grove, Ill.: InterVarsity Press, 1986), pp. 9-85.

22. Callahan *et al., Christianity Divided*, pp. 21-22. Cullmann's article dates from 1953.

23. H. N. Ridderbos, *The Authority of the New Testament Scriptures* (Philadelphia: Presbyterian and Reformed Publishing Co., 1963), pp. 14, 44; cf. G. C. Berkouwer, *Holy Scripture* (Grand Rapids, Mich.: Eerdmans, 1975), pp. 83 ff.

24. On the history of the formation of the New Testament canon, see J. N.

Birdsall, "Canon of the New Testament," in *The New Bible Dictionary*, ed. Douglas, *et al.*; H. N. Ridderbos, "The Canon of the New Testament," in *Revelation and the Bible*, ed. Carl F. H. Henry (Grand Rapids, Mich.: Baker Book House, 1958), pp. 187 ff.; F. F. Bruce, *The Canon of Scripture* (Downers Grove, Ill.: InterVarsity Press, 1988).

25. *Conversations between the Church of England and the Methodist Church* (London: SPCK and Epworth Press, 1963), p. 58 (from the Dissentient View).

26. Rupert E. Davies, *Religious Authority in an Age of Doubt* (London: Epworth Press, 1968), p. 214.

27. In 1951 the volume *Biblical Authority for Today*, ed. A. Richardson and W. Schweizer (Philadelphia: Westminster Press, and London: SCM Press), which the Commission on Faith and Order of the World Council of Churches had sponsored, offered a consensus by fifteen leading biblical scholars on guiding principles for biblical interpretation (pp. 240-44). In 1967 Erich Dinkler concluded his report to the Commission on Faith and Order as follows: "When the World Council of Churches was founded, there was a strong hope . . . that . . . the Bible would be read more and more along the same lines, provided by the development of the so-called 'biblical theology.' Now, two decades later, attention is increasingly drawn to the diversity amongst or even contradiction between biblical writers. . . . As a consequence the hope that the churches would find themselves to have . . . a common understanding of the one biblical message has been fading, even to such an extent that in the eyes of some the new exegetical developments seem to undermine the *raison d'être* of the ecumenical movement" (quoted from Childs, *Biblical Theology in Crisis*, pp. 81-82).

28. See the books listed in note 12 above, and from the Roman Catholic side, see, for instance, L. Bouyer, *The Meaning of Sacred Scripture* (London: Darton, Longman & Todd, 1960; and Notre Dame, Ind.: Univ. of Notre Dame Press, 1958); C. Charlier, *The Christian Approach to the Bible* (London: Sands, 1958).

29. Augustine, *Confessions* 8.29

30. Martin Luther, *Works* (Weimar: Bohlau, 1883-1948), 54.179ff.

31. Journal 24 May 1738, in *Works of John Wesley*, ed. Thomas Jackson (repr. Grand Rapids, Mich.: Baker Book House, 1986) I.103.

32. F. F. Bruce, *Romans*, Tyndale Commentary (London: Tyndale Press, 1963), p. 60.

33. Karl Barth, *Church Dogmatics*, I. i: *The Doctrine of the Word of God*, tr. G. W. Bromiley (Edinburgh: T. & T. Clark, 1975), p. 107; criticized by, e.g., H. Cunliffe-Jones, *The Authority of the Biblical Revelation* (London: James Clarke, 1945), chapter 8.

34. Childs, *Biblical Theology in Crisis*, p. 103.

35. Harold Lindsell, *The Battle for the Bible* (Grand Rapids, Mich.: Zondervan, 1979).

36. The books sponsored by the International Council on Biblical Inerrancy attempted this vindication: see the main items listed in note 14 to chapter 3, p. 244 of this volume.

Chapter 3/A LONG WAR

1. See E. L. Mascall, *Theology and the Gospel of Christ* (London: SPCK, 1977), esp. chap. 1.

2. Calvin *Institutes of the Christian Religion* 1.7.5. For a vigorous assertion of Calvin's view of the Holy Spirit's inner witness as integral to Augustinian and catholic Christian theology, see Alan Richardson, *Christian Apologetics* (London: SCM Press, 1947), pp. 211-20.

3. The sentence is etched on my memory: "I have never seen my Lord Jesus Christ, but He has written me a letter." The reference, alas, I cannot find. The idea of Scripture as a letter from Christ is evidently an extrapolation from the letters to the seven churches (Rev. 2–3).

4. J. I. Packer, *"Fundamentalism" and the Word of God* (London: Inter-Varsity Press; and Grand Rapids, Mich.: Eerdmans, 1958).

5. Gabriel Hebert, *Fundamentalism and the Church of God* (London: SCM Press, 1957). Understandably, in view of the withdrawal of the founders of the Inter-Varsity Fellowship from the Student Christian Movement after 1919 on account of the latter's embrace of theological liberalism, SCM Press has had a continuous interest in publishing attacks on evangelical beliefs about the Bible. *The Doctrine of an Infallible Book* by Charles Gore (1924) was the first such attack, and James Barr's *Fundamentalism* (1977; 2d ed. 1981) and *Escaping from Fundamentalism* (1984) are the most recent.

6. On the idealism and goals of American fundamentalism, see now two brilliant books by George M. Marsden: *Fundamentalism and American Culture: The Shaping of Twentieth Century Evangelicalism, 1870-1925* (New York: Oxford Univ. Press, 1980) and *Reforming Fundamentalism: Fuller Seminary and the New Evangelicalism* (Grand Rapids, Mich.: Eerdmans, 1987).

7. "Prior to 1870, inerrancy, while often assumed, was not used as a test of orthodoxy. But . . . a pivotal episode was the debate in the 1880s and 1890s between Benjamin Warfield and Charles Briggs. . . . Warfield used the inerrancy issue to attack Briggs' moderate revisionism. Once the battle line was so drawn, there was no backing down" (Marsden, *Reforming Fundamentalism*, p. 214). No such battle of the giants occurred in Britain, however, where from 1880 to 1950 a pacific pietism, which lacked altogether the intellectual passion exemplified by Old Princeton, dominated evangelical life. During the 1950s two London ministers, D. M. Lloyd-Jones and John Stott, were influential as revivers of evangelical theological concern in and through Britain's Inter-Varsity Fellowship.

8. This point has been argued by, e.g., Packer, *"Fundamentalism,"* pp. 54-64; J. W. Wenham, *Christ and the Bible* (London: Inter-Varsity Press; and Downers Grove, Ill.: InterVarsity Press, 1973), chap. 1; J. W. Wenham, "Christ's View of Scripture," in *Inerrancy*, ed. Norman L. Geisler, (Grand Rapids, Mich.: Zondervan, 1979), pp. 3-36; cf. Wayne Grudem, "Scripture's Self-attestation and the Problem of Formulating a Doctrine of Scripture," in *Scripture and Truth*, ed. D. A. Carson and John D. Woodbridge (Grand Rapids, Mich.: Zondervan, 1983). Behind these and similar discussions stand Warfield's magisterial analy-

sis, "The Real Problem of Inspiration," in *The Works of Benjamin B. Warfield*, vol. 1 of *Revelation and Inspiration* (Grand Rapids, Mich.: Baker Book House, 1981), pp. 169-226, together with the rest of the material in that volume. See also pp. 36-40 in this volume.

9. Westminster Confession of Faith I. iv.

10. See Marsden, *Reforming Fundamentalism*, chaps. 11-12, and on Wenham, p. 228; Harold Lindsell, *The Battle for the Bible* (Grand Rapids, Mich.: Zondervan, 1976), pp. 106-21, and on Wenham, pp. 131-32; and Roger Nicole in *Doing Theology for the People of God*, ed. Donald Lewis and Alister McGrath (Downers Grove, Ill.: InterVarsity Press, 1996), p. 181.

11. This was the position of Daniel Fuller, who summarily set it forth in "Benjamin B. Warfield's View of Faith and History," *Bulletin of the Evangelical Theological Society* 11(1968): 80-82, and "The Nature of Biblical Inerrancy," *Journal of the American Scientific Affiliation* 24(1972): 47, 50. Clark Pinnock criticized it in his chapter, "Limited Inerrancy," in *God's Inerrant Word*, ed. John Warwick Montgomery (Minneapolis: Bethany Fellowship, 1974), pp. 147-48. It is ironic that, traveling by a different theological route (a revised doctrine of God), Pinnock should now have come to a position that amounts to much the same thing as Fuller's. See Pinnock, *The Scripture Principle* (San Francisco: Harper and Row, 1984), chap. 4, esp. pp. 100-5.

12. Marsden perceptively comments: "The doctrine of inerrancy was . . . functioning at several levels at once. At the most academic level, many conservatives saw it as simply a logically necessary doctrine of the faith. Many progressives, on the other hand, viewed it as confusing, misleading, or simply wrong. But the . . . doctrine also functioned at ecclesiastical and para-ecclesiastical institutional levels. That in turn meant that it was becoming the chief symbol for party division within institutions" (*Reforming Fundamentalism*, p. 227).

13. Cited from a statement prefixed to each item in ICBI's *Foundation Series* of small books.

14. The books included *The Foundation of Biblical Authority*, ed. James M. Boice (Grand Rapids, Mich.: Zondervan, 1978): *Inerrancy* (Papers from Summit 1), ed. Norman L. Geisler (Grand Rapids, Mich.: Zondervan, 1979); *Biblical Inerrancy: Its Philosophical Roots*, ed. Norman L. Geisler (Grand Rapids, Mich.: Zondervan, 1981); Gleason L. Archer, *An Encyclopedia of Bible Difficulties* (Grand Rapids, Mich.: Zondervan, 1982); *Hermeneutics, Inerrancy, and the Bible* (Papers from Summit 2), ed. Earl D. Radmacher and Robert D. Preus (Grand Rapids, Mich.: Zondervan, 1984); *Inerrancy and the Church*, ed. John D. Hannah (Chicago: Moody Press, 1984); *Challenges to Inerrancy: A Theological Response*, ed. Gordon Lewis and Bruce Demarest (Chicago: Moody Press, 1984); *Applying the Scriptures* (Papers from Summit 3), ed. Kenneth S. Kantzer (Grand Rapids, Mich.: Zondervan, 1987). The consensus statements from the first two summits, with exposition, were reprinted as appendixes to my book *God Has Spoken* (Grand Rapids, Mich.: Baker Book House, 1988). "A Short Statement" from Summit 1 (1978) is reproduced as an appendix to this chapter (see p. 124).

15. From his speech at ICBI's final activity, the 1987 Congress on the Bible in Washington, D.C.: James M. Boice, ed., *Transforming Our World* (Portland, Ore.: Multnomah Press, 1988), p. 11. All the speeches were reprinted in this volume. ICBI's intiatives have prompted some valuable seminary-sponsored symposia on the inerrancy question: Roger R. Nicole and J. Ramsey Michaels, eds., *Inerrancy and Common Sense* (Grand Rapids, Mich.: Baker Book House, 1980); D. A. Carson and John D. Woodbridge, eds., *Scripture and Truth* (Grand Rapids, Mich.: Zondervan, 1983); Carson and Woodbridge, *Hermeneutics, Authority and Canon* (Grand Rapids, Mich.: Zondervan, 1986); Harvie M. Conn, ed., *Inerrancy and Hermeneutic* (Grand Rapids, Mich.: Baker Book House, 1988).

16. See esp. John D. Woodbridge, *Biblical Authority: A Critique of the Rogers and McKim Proposal* (Grand Rapids, Mich.: Zondervan, 1982). Jack Rogers—joint-author with Donald McKim of *The Authority and Interpretation of the Bible: An Historical Approach* (San Francisco: Harper and Row, 1979), a large and uneven special plea for a noninerrantist, functionalist view of biblical authority as warranted by the best patristic and Protestant precedents—was a leading Fuller Seminary professor. My estimate of this work is given in J. I. Packer, *Beyond the Battle for the Bible* (Westchester, Ill.: Crossway, 1980), pp. 146-51.

17. See Douglas Johnson, *Contending for the Faith* (Leicester, Eng.: Inter-Varsity Press, 1979), pp. 209-13, 297-99; Geraint Fielder, *Lord of the Years* (Leicester, Eng.: Inter-Varsity Press, 1988), pp. 82ff.

18. See Marsden, *Reforming Fundamentalism*, chaps. 1–3.

19. Richard F. Lovelace, *Dynamics of Spiritual Life: An Evangelical Theology of Renewal* (Downers Grove, Ill.: InterVarsity Press, 1979), pp. 11-12; John White, *When the Spirit Comes with Power: Signs and Wonders Among God's People* (Downers Grove, Ill.: InterVarsity Press, 1988), esp. chap. 16.

20. Mark Noll, *Between Faith and Criticism: Evangelicals, Scholarship, and the Bible in America* (San Francisco: Harper and Row, 1987), pp. 131-37.

21. To avoid misunderstanding, let it be said that *criticism* and *critical*, as applied to biblical study, have become systematically ambiguous words. If *biblical criticism* is defined as answering questions about the date, place, sources, background, literary character, credentials, and purpose of each composition, all evangelicals practice it. If it is defined as affirming answers to these questions that imply untrustworthiness or fraudulence of any kind in the documents, all evangelicals oppose it. Whether particular evangelicals profess to accept or oppose biblical criticism thus depends on how they define it. My use of the term here is in the former sense.

22. The phrase *analogy of faith* stands for the principle of interpreting Scripture harmoniously, letting what is basic and clear illuminate what is peripheral and obscure. The procedure assumes that, inasmuch as all Scripture proceeds ultimately from a single mind, that of God, intrinsic coherence is there to be discovered in the biblical material. Biblical exploration over two millennia has shown that this heuristic principle is every bit as viable as is the denial of it. But in nonevangelical Protestantism today the assumption of coherence is lacking, and the discipline of "biblical theology" has consequently lost its way. See, for

evidence of this, Brevard S. Childs, *Biblical Theology in Crisis* (Philadelphia: Westminster Press, 1970).

23. See Edmund P. Clowney, *Preaching and Biblical Theology* (London: Inter-Varsity Press; and Grand Rapids, Mich.: Eerdmans, 1961); and for a sample of the discipline in action, see his book *The Unfolding Mystery: Discovering Christ in the Old Testament* (Colorado Springs: NavPress, 1988). Australian authors who have led the way in biblical theology include W. J. Dumbrell, *Covenant and Creation: An Old Testament Covenantal Theology* (Homebush West: Lancer; and Exeter: Paternoster Press, 1984); *The End of the Beginning* (Homebush West: Lancer; and Grand Rapids, Mich.: Baker Book House, 1985); *The Search for Order* (Grand Rapids, Mich.: Baker, 1994); Graeme Goldsworthy, *According to Plan* (Homebush West: Lancer; and Leicester: Inter-Varsity Press, 1991).

24. Sample writings: Sir Edwyn C. Hoskyns and Francis Noel Davey, *The Riddle of the New Testament* (London: Faber and Faber, 1947); Gabriel Hebert, *The Throne of David* (London: Faber and Faber, 1941); H. H. Rowley, *The Relevance of the Bible* (New York: Macmillan, 1943); Rowley, *The Rediscovery of the Old Testament* (Philadelphia: Westminster Press, 1946); Rowley, *The Unity of the Bible* (Philadelphia: Westminster Press, 1955); Alan Richardson, *The Miracle-Stories of the Gospels* (London: SCM Press, 1941); A. M. Hunter, *The Message of the New Testament* (Philadelphia: Westminster Press, 1944), previously published as *The Unity of the New Testament* (London: SCM Press, 1943); G. Ernest Wright and Reginald H. Fuller, *The Book of the Acts of God* (New York: Doubleday, 1957); Floyd V. Filson, *The New Testament Against Its Environment* (London: SCM Press, 1950); James D. Smart, *The Interpretation of Scripture* (Philadelphia: Westminster Press, 1961); Smart, *The Strange Silence of the Bible in the Church* (Philadelphia: Westminster Press, 1970); Smart, *The Past, Present, and Future of Biblical Theology* (Philadelphia: Westminster Press, 1979); Krister Stendahl, "Biblical Theology, Contemporary," in *The Interpreter's Dictionary of the Bible* (Nashville: Abingdon Press, 1962) 1:418-32; Paul Minear, *Images of the Church in the New Testament* (Philadelphia: Westminster Press, 1960); Millar Burrows, *An Outline of Biblical Theology* (Philadelphia: Westminster Press, 1946); Bernhard W. Anderson, *The Unfolding Drama of the Bible* (New York: Association Press, 1957).

25. Compare the (probably apocryphal) remark ascribed to Julius Wellhausen about the teaching of W. Robertson Smith and his supporters (Smith lost his chair at the Free Church College, Aberdeen, for teaching higher criticism in a way that was held to undermine faith in biblical inspiration, though Smith denied that it did): "I knew the Old Testament was a fraud, but I never thought anyone would make God party to it, as these Scotsmen are doing."

26. Klaus Bockmuehl, in *The Unreal God of Modern Theology* (Colorado Springs: Helmers and Howard, 1988), castigates the theological version of this double-talk as it deserves; see esp. chap. 4, "The Collapse of the Doctrine of God."

27. James Barr, who specializes in demolition work, took the lead here. See his *The Semantics of Biblical Language* (London: Oxford Univ. Press, 1961); "Revelation through History in the Old Testament and in Modern Theology," *Inter-*

pretation 17 (1963): 193-205; *Old and New in Interpretation* (London: SCM Press; New York: Harper and Row, 1966).

28. See Brevard S. Childs, *Biblical Theology in Crisis* (Philadelphia: Westminster Press, 1970), pp. 51-87.

29. Gerhard Kittel's massive enterprise, *Theological Dictionary of the New Testament*, 9 vols., 1938-73, trans. Geoffrey W. Bromiley (Grand Rapids, Mich.: Eerdmans, 1964-74), was sparked by the new interest in Scripture that neo-orthodoxy was generating and out of which "biblical theology" was to emerge. Other ventures, modeled on Kittel, include Colin Brown, ed., *New International Dictionary of New Testament Theology*, 3 vols. (Grand Rapids, Mich.: Eerdmans, 1975-78); J. J. Von Allmen, *Vocabulary of the Bible* (London: Lutterworth, 1958); and the theological entries in many modern Bible dictionaries.

30. See Roger Nicole's assessment in Gordon Lewis and Bruce Demarest, eds., *Challenges to Inerrancy* (Chicago: Moody Press, 1984), pp. 122-36.

31. See J. I. Packer in Bruce Kaye and Gordon Wenham, eds., *Law, Morality, and the Bible* (Downers Grove, Ill.: InterVarsity Press, 1978), pp. 154-55. "Theological contextualism" is the description of Barth's ethics by G. Outka, *Agape: An Ethical Analysis* (New Haven: Yale University Press, 1972), pp. 229ff.

32. For detailed biblical assessment of Barth's distinctive positions, see G. C. Berkouwer, *The Triumph of Grace in the Theology of Karl Barth* (Grand Rapids, Mich.: Eerdmans, 1956) and Colin Brown, *Karl Barth and the Christian Message* (London: Tyndale Press, 1967).

33. R. H. Roberts, in S. W. Sykes, ed., *Karl Barth* (Oxford: Clarendon Press, 1979), p. 145.

34. "The effect of [Bultmann's] work is to *reduce* the content of Christian theology to a single idea: that of the act or decision in which man draws his self-understanding and thus his self into conformity with his authentic being as potentiality to be." Robert C. Roberts, *Rudolf Bultmann's Theology: A Critical Interpretation* (Grand Rapids, Mich.: Eerdmans, 1976), p. 323.

35. Space forbade any discussion of contemporary Roman Catholic treatment of the Bible; but see my comments in Boice, *The Foundation of Biblical Authority*, pp. 74ff.; also John Warwick Montgomery, "The Approach of New Shape Roman Catholicism to Scriptural Inerrancy: A Case Study for Evangelicals," in *Ecumenicity, Evangelicals, and Rome* (Grand Rapids, Mich.: Zondervan, 1969).

Chapter 5/MOUTHPIECE FOR GOD

1. C. S. Lewis, *The Problem of Pain* (London: Geoffrey Bles, 1940), preface, p. vii.

2. Now published as *The Heart of the Gospel*, ed. Christopher Catherwood (Eastbourne: Crossway Books, 1991).

3. W. H. Griffith Thomas, *The Work of the Ministry* (London: Hodder & Stoughton, 1911); cited in Warren W. Wiersbe, "Introduction to the Author," in W. H. Griffith Thomas, *The Apostle Peter* (Grand Rapids, Mich.: Kregel Publications, 1984), p. (9).

4. Abner Brown, *Recollections of the Conversation Parties of the Revd. Charles Simeon* (N.p., 1863), p. 126.

5. Richard Baxter, *The Reformed Pastor* (Edinburgh: Banner of Truth, 1974), pp. 61ff.

6. On the Holy Spirit in preaching, see further D. M. Lloyd-Jones, *Preachers and Preaching* (London: Hodder & Stoughton, 1971; Grand Rapids, Mich.: Zondervan, 1972), chap. 5, "The Act of Preaching," pp. 81-99; and Tony Sargent, *The Sacred Anointing: The Preaching of Dr. Martyn Lloyd-Jones* (London: Hodder & Stoughton, 1994).

7. Richard Baxter, *A Christian Directory* (Morgan, Penn.: Soli Deo Gloria, 1996), pp. 473-77.

SCRIPTURE INDEX